I C

by

Samuel Reilly

A Memory of National Service

1950 – 1952

THE ROYAL AIRFORCE

Dedicated to all those National Servicemen who served their country in some form or other.

And who, at some time in their service, would be told to "get some in" (service that is) by their old heads who, according to them, had "GOT SOME IN" and get their knees brown if they were overseas!

CHAPTER ONE

THE DREADED CALL UP

I got some in when I was called up in July 1950, just a month after my 18th birthday.

This induced panic in my mother whom you will discover was very protective of my sister and me. Now, within a few short months, we would both fly the nest. My sister married, and me serving King and Country.

We had been on holiday in Ireland and came back to find my call up papers behind the door. Right away my mother started to make arrangements to send me straight back to Ireland where there was no National Service. The small matter of me having to spend at least five years there before I could come back hadn't occurred to her; and, even then, there was no guarantee I wouldn't be prosecuted for dodging National Service.

I turned down her offer of a one-way ticket to Ireland but this didn't put her off. Without me knowing, she contacted our GP and told him I was far too delicate to be called up on the basis that I had had a serious illness when I was five and didn't go to school until I was six and had been unwell ever since. Not true as far as I was concerned! I had a happy healthy childhood despite my mother's attempts to stop me doing all the things normal, healthy children did. Needless to say, the doctor was having none of it and my father agreed with him too. Having fought in the First World War and serving well into the 1930s with the TA, the only thing that prevented him from being in the Second World War was that he was too old!

CHAPTER TWO

THE MEDICAL

Shortly after I received my papers I was invited to attend a medical at a school in the centre of Glasgow.

We were met by an array of doctors who proceeded to examine us as to our suitability for service in the forces. The children's song, "Heads, shoulders, knees and toes; eyes and ears and mouth and nose," summed the whole thing up very well. The fact that you were standing about in your underwear for quite some time didn't seem to bother the doctors as much as it did us. Then came the dreaded 'cough' where you had to drop your trousers and cough while some stranger held a part of your anatomy that you would rather had not been grabbed! I never understood the reason for this although I think it had something to do with having a hernia.

The medical complete, we were ushered to a classroom to undertake an aptitude test. Before the test began we were spoken to by someone who explained the various tests and how long we would have to complete them. He then said that anyone who had a preference for the RAF would have to be pretty good as "they only take the 'crème de la crème'." So, no pressure then!

The stopwatch started and we had to fill in our personal details plus any interests, hobbies and membership of any youth groups. The lad next to me was sat staring at his form for ages after writing his name and address. Finally he turned to me and said, "How do you spell Boys Brigade?"

"Just put BB in capital letters," I whispered to him. Next we had some spelling, maths and English tests and then it was over. We were told to wait outside for our results.

We were then taken in one by one and I was told I was Grade 1 and had been accepted for the Royal Air Force, much to my mother's horror and surprise. It was no surprise to me as I considered myself very fit.

I had played football, tennis, badminton, table tennis and was an active member of a rowing club, training three times a week and taking part in regattas every weekend during the summer. So, yes, I thought I was pretty fit! Until I got to RAF Hereford to do my basic training that is, but much more of that later!

I met up with the lad who had sat beside me at the tests.

"How did you get on?" he asked.

I told him that I had passed Grade 1. "How about you?" I asked.

"Grade 4," he said. "What does that mean?"

I hadn't the heart to tell him he had failed and wouldn't be going anywhere. Perhaps he was the lucky one. Who knows?

Shortly afterwards I received my instructions to report to RAF Padgate at 06.00 hours on 31st October 1950. Yes, it was Halloween and that should have alerted me to the horrors that awaited me. Very thoughtfully they had included a Travel Warrant for me to get there, not first class of course!

Padgate? I hadn't a clue where it was. Somewhere in the Midlands, I was told. My Dad came to see me off at Glasgow Central Station to catch the ten o'clock train to London, stopping at Carlisle, Crewe, etc. - you know the drill. My Dad was a man of very few words and even now I couldn't tell you much about his time in the army. He was a Regimental Sergeant Major and didn't I know it! That said, he was hard but fair. The only advice he offered me was: "Keep in with the man who feeds you, the man who clothes you and the man who pays you and you won't go far wrong."

I managed to find a seat in the busy train. In the compartment were an American airman and his wife. After we left Carlisle I opened my packed lunch, prepared of course by my mother! Along with the usual sandwiches she had packed a large red apple. When the airman's wife saw it she said, "I haven't seen an apple like that since I left the States." I offered her the apple and she accepted it with thanks.

The airman picked up what I had thought was a briefcase, but when he opened it, it was packed with miniature bottles of whiskey and brandy which he proceeded to force on me during the rest of the journey in return for giving his wife the apple!

By the time I got to Padgate I was rather squiffy, but all that changed and I soon sobered up when I met my reception committee!

CHAPTER THREE

PADGATE

I arrived at Padgate Station at 05.30 hours. (See how easy it is to pick up the lingo? I'd never heard of the 24-hour clock before!) I waited outside the station, joined now by about six other lads. I had noticed this most peculiar smell and couldn't place it. The smell, coupled with a cold damp morning and the sight of huge buildings surrounded by massive tanks, gave the place an eerie, futuristic feel. I mentioned the smell, which was pretty powerful, and was told it was coming from the soap works which were the main industry in the town. Unilever - the home of Sunlight Soap and makers of various soap powders - employed a lot of people. Little did I know that when I got to RAF Stafford I would meet one of the Unilever heirs.

At about six o'clock a wagon pulled up painted Air Force blue with the RAF Roundels on it. A corporal and an airman opened and lowered the tail gate of the garrie, as the wagons were called. To this day I don't know why. We were invited to climb aboard, or rather told to get our arses up there! I can't say the journey was comfortable as the seats were wooden benches and you felt every bump in the road. Plus we were thrown about and had to hold on to the sides of the wagon and each other! Talk about 'Health and Safety'!

The journey thankfully didn't take long and, again, we were invited to get our arses off the wagon and form two ranks, "at the double," naturally.

My first impression of Padgate was a sprawl of missen huts, a cook house and not much more. This, and others like it, was to be my home for the next eighteen months – correction - the next two years, because the Korean War had just started. Someone in their wisdom decided to add another six months on to the National Service and we would be among the first intakes to enjoy an extra six months at "His Majesty's Pleasure." Was I grateful? No I was not!

We were marched to our billet. Well, I say marched. Some of us did, others didn't. Two or three marched like ducks – left, left, right, right, arms straight out in front - the bane of Drill Instructors, who described them as pregnant ducks! I was lucky I had been in the Air Training Corps and knew a little about drill and how to handle a rifle. Smart Alec, but I would soon be taken down a peg or two! We were told this was a transit camp and we would be kitted out here and then be posted elsewhere for basic training.

CHAPTER FOUR

GET YOUR KIT ON

We were (you guessed it) marched to the stores to be kitted out. This entailed waiting at a long counter behind which were various store men who would throw items of clothing at you, ignoring any attempt to tell them what size you were. To be fair, they had long experience in the job and were probably right nine times out of ten. Shoes (oh yes, shoes for best uniform), not like the Army who wore boots all the time and also boots for drill and work. They did take heed of your size for those. Not so hats. They couldn't find a beret small enough for me and had to issue me with a forage cap, which they were trying to phase out. Why I do not know. I think caps looked far better on than berets any day; apart from the Marines and Paras who always looked smart to me. Nowadays the RAF wear the modern skipped cap. Very smart!

I had to have a chit issued giving me permission to wear the forage cap, much to the annoyance of many NCOs and officials. In hindsight I was left wide open to be picked on because of my outdated headwear. After we were issued with our kit - "Airmen for the use of" - and a kit bag to store it in, we had to stencil our number on every item of clothing and also stamp our number on our 'irons,' i.e. knife, fork, spoon, along with a mug for tea (not purple, that's another story) which you had to guard with your life. Wages were 13/6 a week, which is 67½ pence in today's money and lost items of kit were expensive, plus you were likely to be put on a charge if kit went missing.

So now I was officially for the next two years 3130146 Aircraftsman Second Class Reilly S. and the adventure continues. After we were kitted out, we were issued with our bedding. Three biscuits (bits of mattress put together to form a single bed), blankets (two), sheets (two), airmen for the use of.

CHAPTER FIVE

MY FIRST RAF MEAL

After being kitted out, we were treated to our first RAF dinner – sausage, beans and mashed potatoes, followed by semolina pudding (ugh, pass the sick bag!). Holding my very new plate I was given two sausages, beans and then the lad made an attempt to deposit mashed potatoes on my plate. After three tries he finally slammed the utensil down and smashed the plate in two; and then glared at me as if it were my fault! Sausages were to play a further part in my RAF life but you will have to wait until we get to RAF Stafford to hear more.

CHAPTER SIX

WHO'S THAT GHOST?

My first night sleeping in a billet with forty-two other people was a new experience and turned out to be quite scary. Apparently some Airman had hanged himself in the very billet we were in. Whether this was true or just an attempt to scare us witless, it actually worked. Especially for one chap, a young Scots lad from Aberdeen. A fine featured, fair haired boy.

It must have been about three o'clock in the morning. The billet was in darkness. Lights out at 21.30 hours. There was a full moon shining in the window straight on to his bed space giving him a spectral glow! I awoke to the sound of him wailing like a banshee.

"There he is," he wailed, "the lad who hanged himself. He's coming in the windae." He was pointing straight at the window behind me, or 'windae' as he called it with his Aberdonian twang. I am not easily frightened, but I surely was that morning. Turned out the poor lad was having a nightmare and it took a lot of convincing to assure him it was nothing more than that. We stayed a few more days at Padgate and then we were paraded and given our training postings. 31131046 Reilly S. to Hereford, home to the RAF Regiment (now home to the S.A.S), who would be in charge of our weapons training and unarmed combat.

CHAPTER SEVEN

RAF HEREFORD: LET THE TORTURE BEGIN

We were back to the old mantra. Everything done "at the double": run to lectures, run to meals, P.E., drill and even run to get a haircut. After a week of this however, we settled down to a more civilised march. We were introduced to a lovely man, Corporal Jones by name. As you would guess Welsh by nature and beast by choice!

His first task was to go around the billets asking us our names and where we came from. Then he picked on the smallest lad in the Flight ('F' Flight as it happens).

"Do you like me, Sammy?" he asked in a rather reasonable voice.

"Yes, Corporal," came the reply.

"You rotten stinking liar!" he screamed. "You don't even know me. I don't like you and by the time I'm finished with you lot, none of you will like me." He was not wrong. Then he spoke to me. "I see by your number you were in the ATC."

"I was," I said.

"Good," he said. "You will get certain favours, starting with you taking charge of my webbing and blancoing, and polishing it every night for eight weeks." Then he dropped a bigger bombshell. "Because of the Korean War, your training has been extended from eight weeks to sixteen weeks." Oh joy! Sixteen weeks with him and the other monsters. I did his webbing for a few nights and then another lad came up with a brilliant idea. There were two fire buckets at the top of the billet. So, seeing me trying to cope with my own kit and that of Corporal Jones, he took the corporal's kit off me, dropped it in a fire bucket and hung it up to dry. I must say it didn't half look bad and I only had to blanco and brasso a few times to keep it up to scratch. In fact, at the end of our "square bashing," Corporal Jones congratulated me on a job well done. Little did he know!

CHAPTER EIGHT

SEX SHOCK!

Our first introduction to our training came in the form of a film entitled, "An introduction to V.D. (Venereal Disease)". In my teens I was interested in girls, but as sport took up a lot of my time I was never in what people would call today a serious relationship. We went out in a mixed crowd and enjoyed each other's company, but sex was off the menu. After watching this horror film, sex was definitely off the menu! Added to this of course was the fact that, without our knowledge, we had bromide added to our tea, thereby limiting any amount of libido we had in the first place.

Every day was now taken up with drill, marching and rifle drill and, like our first days at RAF Padgate, we had our share of pregnant ducks, not so much marching as waddling. This used to drive the drill instructors mad and leave them red in the face with rage. Of course, anybody who thought it was funny and laughed or tittered would be sent around the square several times with their rifle over their head. The laughing soon stopped after a few sessions of this!

CHAPTER NINE

JOHN WAYNE, STEP FORWARD

My nemesis was a corporal from Yorkshire who took a great delight in calling me "Reely," despite being told a few times it was Reilly. You soon caught on to when you were being wound up and, if you were smart, you ignored it.

However I had to laugh one morning on parade. The corporal stood there with his drill stick tapping away and calling, "You there, John Wayne," to which everybody, including me, didn't respond. He repeated himself, moving down the ranks until his face was level with mine. "You're John Wayne," he said. Flattered though I was to be likened to a famous cowboy, I couldn't see the resemblance myself, John Wayne being 6' 2" plus, and me only 5' 8" and weighing in at a massive 8 stone 7 pounds. However, the connection soon became clear. I had been chewing gum before I went on parade and still had it in my mouth, chewing away unawares, hence "John Wayne", I suppose after the habit of cowboys chewing tobacco in the western films. Surprisingly, the corporal didn't take the matter further and I didn't fall foul of him again until a few weeks later.

Every day on parade the Flight Sergeant would come behind the recruits and when his hand fell on your shoulder you were told to get a haircut. This despite the fact that we all had short back and sides from day one. No one escaped and when it happened to me I couldn't believe what happened next.

I went to the barber who, without asking why I was there, went through the motions of cutting my hair. No sooner had I got outside along with three or four other recruits, we were told to get a haircut again despite the fact that we had just had one that we didn't really need in the first place! This happened to me twice. The third time I caught on to the game. If you were last getting back to the barber you had to have another haircut. The others before you were let off. This time I made sure I wasn't last and the ordeal was over.

CHAPTER TEN

PAY UP OR ELSE!

It was amazing the ways in which the RAF had of separating you from your money. Apart from the haircut scam, they had a system in place called "Barrack Room Damages," whereby any damage, in their opinion, done to fittings and fixtures had to be paid for.

In all the time we were stationed at RAF Hereford I cannot recall any damage being done apart from a spare locker, but more of that later. However, we were docked 1/6 (7 ½ pence) per week for every week we were there for a chipped lampshade which was already chipped when we got there! A nice little earner, as Arthur Daley would have said! No amount of protesting was listened to and no attempt was made to replace the lamp shade during our stay there.

CHAPTER ELEVEN

KILL OR BE KILLED

The daily grind of drill, unarmed combat training, P.E. and lectures continued as it would every day for the next sixteen weeks. Every day we were marched to a large hanger type building where we did our weapons and unarmed combat training. All around the walls were paintings of Korean soldiers six feet tall with very grim expressions on their faces and captions underneath stating: "Kill or be killed"; "It's him or you"; "Hesitate with your bayonet and you're dead."

Seeing those images every day for such a long time stayed with me for quite a while. This coupled with the training on how to kill using no weapons had a lasting effect.

I was married six years after National Service and, one day, my new wife ran out of the kitchen and, in fun, jumped on to my back. Without thinking, I sent her flying forward over my shoulder and she landed on her back on the floor. I couldn't convince her that, even after six years, old habits die hard. Then again, I would gladly have killed a Korean soldier given the chance after all the brainwashing we had because that's what it was - and it worked. Ask my wife!

CHAPTER TWELVE

CARRY ON TEACHING

The lectures continued and one day after a session of drill and P.E. I fell asleep during a lecture on tank warfare. What that had to do with the RAF I don't know, but then again we were told over and over again by the instructors, "You lot are going to Korea," which did little to cheer us all up. Hence the reason for the longer training.

The room was very hot and stuffy. One minute I was watching tanks and infantry, the next I was being prodded awake by an officer's swagger stick.

"Since you were asleep young man, perhaps you would like to change places and carry on where I have left off." At last, an officer with a sense of humour! I felt myself warming to him. Of course I couldn't carry on where he had left off, not having a clue about any of it. Apparently I only came to his attention in the dark because I began snoring. To his credit he let me off. Even he was bored with the whole thing!

CHAPTER THIRTEEN

GAS MASKS ON, GAS MASKS OFF

Just to relive the monotony of drill, lectures, etc, we had the delight of the Gas Chamber. This was a device to give you an idea of what to expect during a gas attack. You paraded in full kit complete with cape and gas mask. The idea was that you entered the chamber with your gas mask on. Crystals were then broken and the gas released. The order would then come: "Gas masks off," and you had to inhale the gas to give you the impression of a gas attack. My friend, who had a somewhat scientific nature, came up with a "cunning plan" (long before Baldrick) and worked out that with forty-two airmen, if we could be the last two in there wouldn't be a lot of gas left.

Talk about the best laid plans, etc.; we were told to put our masks on and no talking. However, we were so busy hatching our cunning plan we didn't realise that we were being observed. We should have known better. We were always being observed. We got the dreaded tap on the shoulder and invited to jump forty places to the front of the queue and therefore be first in (thanks mate!). We entered the gas chamber and were then told: "Gas masks off." It wasn't too bad at first and then – wham - the full effects on the eyes were felt. People tried to put their masks back on, but we were made to keep them off for what seemed like ages, although it probably wasn't. We were then told to put our masks back on and then we had to go outside and run one hundred yards in full kit with our gas masks still on and then take them off. The minute the air hit us we were as sick as dogs, much to the amusement of the NCOs and officers. We were not amused!

CHAPTER FOURTEEN

THESE BOOTS WERE MADE FOR MARCHING

The other little treat the officers had in store for us, apart from the assault course which came in our final week, was to march us in full kit to Gredon Hill, a mountain about five miles from camp. Gredon Hill was also the name of the base, RAF Gredon Hill. The Welsh called them mountains, but being very Scottish, I wasn't impressed! I would have said "Brecon Hills" but, hey, what do I know! All I do know is that by now I was beginning to realise just how unfit I was after thinking I was super fit, having taken part in all the sporting activities back home. But back to Gredon Hill.

Halfway up the hill (or halfway down) there was a pub set back off the road. We were halted outside, dismissed and told to: "Go and have a drink, lads. Enjoy yourselves." Surely these were not the same bullying corporals who had made our lives a misery all this time? Everybody piled into the pub and ordered a drink, paid for it and before anyone could even take a sip, we were told to get outside "at the double" and marched straight back to camp. We should have known leopards don't change their spots, or corporals their stripes! The next time they tried it, nobody moved. Their little game was up for the time being.

To be honest though, their behaviour was nothing compared to the corporal in the next billet. Lucas by name and mad by nature, hence the name "Mad Lucas."

I happened to meet a lad that went to the same youth club in Glasgow and he asked me to call round for a chat. When I got there they were all busy cleaning and polishing and cleaning windows (as you do). I managed to talk to him for a few minutes but it was nearly time for lights out. I was about to leave the billet when the corporal appeared and ordered everyone to line up, march around the billet and say goodnight to the fire buckets.

I tried to leave, but I was told, "You're going nowhere until you say goodnight." Needless to say I didn't go back to see the lad again as I had no desire to cut the grass with nail scissors, which he had his lot doing or painting stones white. You know the old saying, if it moves, salute it, if it doesn't, paint it. Very true in service times.

CHAPTER FIFTEEN

BULL-SHIT BAFFLES BRAINS

The endless bull-shit was very wearing and it became quite tiresome polishing the floor two or three times a day only to be told, "Do it again, it's filthy. Do you live in a pig sty at home?"

Beds had to be arranged exactly in line and made up: a blanket, a sheet, a blanket, a sheet and a folded blanket wrapped around the whole lot and squared off. God help you if it wasn't right. The whole lot would be tipped up and you had to start again.

Even the lockers weren't safe. Your clothes had to be folded; even your socks had to be rolled up. Your packs had to be placed neatly on the shelf above your bed and squared off. We had kit inspection on a regular basis. Your kit had to be laid out in a certain way and if it wasn't, up in the air the whole lot would go and you were told that you would be put on a charge, although I don't remember that ever actually happening. After all, there was no point in confining people to barracks because we weren't allowed out of camp anyway. That would come later at RAF Stafford. It was nearly Christmas before we were considered civilised enough to mingle with the local people of Hereford. Before we were let out we had to undergo an inspection by the RAF Police at the guardroom to make sure we were clean, shaved, haircut, uniform polished, buttons polished and shoes gleaming. Anything less than that and you were going nowhere!

CHAPTER SIXTEEN

THE GREAT PEA INCIDENT

In the middle of our training, we were assigned "Fatigue Duties." Some carried out maintenance tasks like painting stones, shovelling coal or other jobs around the camp. I was assigned to the cook house for a week to help prepare and serve the dinners at five o'clock each evening. Compared to other lads, this was a cushy number. The cook house was warm and dry whilst outside it was freezing cold and there was a good six inches of snow on the ground.

There were several large boilers on the floor filled with potatoes, peas, carrots and cabbage, all simmering away. These all had beautiful copper lids and looked most impressive. Our job was to make sure that the boilers didn't dry out and to let the cook know if they needed topping up. This was to keep us occupied until it was time to serve the dinners. The lads in the cook house were easy going and didn't mind a bit of banter. However, my nemesis turned up, accompanied by an Irish corporal who was in charge of the cook house. He said something to the corporal, who then approached me and said, "If you can stand around talking, I'll find you a job to do." He then told me to go to the store room and fetch two or three yellow dusters and a very large tin of "Brasso, Airmen for the use of." He then told me to polish the copper lids on the boilers until they were gleaming - or else. Oh, don't you just love the Irish sense of humour?

Because of the amount of steam it was impossible to polish the lids. Of course they knew this but it gave them a good laugh watching me try. As it was nearly five o'clock and time for dinner, they gave up and wandered off. I had placed the giant Brasso tin on the edge of one of the boilers. Calamity struck as I turned to comment to the lad next to me about the Irish corporal.

My elbow caught the tin of Brasso and in it plopped - into the boiler full of peas! There was the tin with all the Brasso bubbling away among the peas. Panic stricken, I tried to fish it out with a long piece of wire. Eventually I got it, but by this time all the paint had come off, including the lettering declaring: "Property of the W.D." (War Department). I smuggled it outside and put it in the dustbin and so to dinner. As my only witness thought it hilarious, we kept quiet and made a mental note not to have peas with our dinner!

Dinner was served and we watched in amazement as all those bods were happily eating their peas and making no comment. Either the Brasso had added to the flavour, or these guys had stomachs like dustbins. The latter I think. I lived in terror for the next twenty-four hours waiting to see what effect the poison peas would have. None, it seemed and I had to laugh when my co-conspirator said, "I hope they don't blow off or they'll burn their bloody shirt tails off!" The rest of the week passed without further ado.

On the Friday the Corporal Cook took us to help ourselves to the left over pork pies and some butter, which I knew my mother would appreciate (the butter that is). I am afraid I over-indulged on the pork pies and made myself very ill. It was some years before I could look a pork pie in the eye again.

That was the Brasso incident. When we got to Stafford there would be the purple tea incident, but more of that later.

Ah, the wonderful gift of that butter though was to send me into another panic! We had a billet inspection on a regular basis. I had stored the butter in my large pack as I was going on leave the following week and thought I was safe. That was until the billet inspection. In came a very pompous officer aided and abetted by a Flight Sergeant. He had a very close look at everything and you could see that he was getting annoyed at not being able to find fault. He looked up the shelves which held our packs and his eyes alighted on mine. "There is a good example of a well squared off pack,

Flight Sergeant," he commented. "What have you got in there, lad? Bricks?" He then proceeded to wallop the pack with his swagger stick.

Please don't ask me to open it, I prayed. If that butter had been found I would be for the high jump and would have had a hard job of proving I hadn't stolen it. Mercifully he gave up and left and the butter made it safely back to Glasgow.

CHAPTER SEVENTEEN

FLYING OFFICER

On the subject of billet inspections, the winter of 1950 was very severe and a shortage of coke for the stove in the billet made it necessary to look for alternative fuel. There was a spare locker at the top of the billet and one of our enterprising lads thought it would be a good idea to burn it. Horrified at the very thought, we all said no. It would be missed at an inspection and we would all end up paying for it at the very least.

A compromise was reached and it was agreed that we would take the drawer fronts off and burn the drawer carcasses. Job done! If only. Sure enough I was billet orderly on the day of the next inspection. The usual format took place and the officer seemed satisfied. Then he spotted the spare locker. "What's in there, airman?" he asked.

"Nothing, I assure you Sir," said I.

"Well, let's see then," he said, before gripping the top drawer front and pulling hard. I must say it was a credit to all our bull-shit polishing the floor. It was like a skating rink. I will never forget the sight of that officer (he was a Pilot Officer, not a flying one, but he was one that day). He flew down the billet floor on his back whilst the Flight Sergeant and I tried our best not to collapse with laughter. Needless to say we had to pay Barrack Room damages, all in the cause of trying to keep warm, but it was worth it to see the pompous brought down to earth!

CHAPTER EIGHTEEN

NOT TOO CLEAN

Hygiene played a large part during our training, for most of us, that is, with the exception of two people, one who just wouldn't wash and the other who thought filling a sink to the top with hot water and dipping his fingers into it before rubbing his eyes passed for a wash. And he went to bed in full uniform, complete with his boots on.

The other one just stank and it was obvious the forces life was not for him. He was an intelligent lad, but was always in trouble for not obeying orders. The final straw came when Corporal Jones had had enough and, together with the other corporals and our Flight Sergeant, forcibly stripped him and put him in the shower to scrub him clean. I can still hear his screams now! Strangely we never saw him again after that, but it was a wakeup call for our Cockney wide boy and he started to wash properly, instead of wasting hot water, which was scarce at the best of times.

CHAPTER NINETEEN

MEET THE BUTCHER

I suppose dentistry comes under the banner of hygiene, oral that is. Due to go on leave the following week, I developed toothache, but was determined to wait until I got home to have it looked at. But fate was not on my side.

The Flight Sergeant looked in, took one look at my swollen face and said, "Dentist, lad."

"I can't, Flight," I said. "I'm the billet orderly." Everyone had to take a turn of billet orderly to ensure security.

"Don't worry, I'll sort that out," Flight said. "Off you go to the dentist."

Oh what joy, just what I needed. I had heard all the tales about the camp butcher. Taking out the wrong tooth, lads covered in blood and the dentist covered in blood too. Whether the stories were true or not, I was about to find out.

I rang the surgery bell and was greeted by a massive size of a man. "Come in and sit up on the chair, let me have a look."

He looked in my mouth and, being helpful, I said, "It's this one."

"Now now," said he. "Don't spoil the fun. Let me find it."

We're off to a good start, thought I.

He tapped the bad tooth and I jumped in agony. "I'll just inject your gum with this new drug and we will find out if it works or not." Now I was a guinea pig. "Just sit out there for ten minutes and I'll call you back in." Ten minutes later he called me back in and jabbed a needle in my gum. "Anything?" he asked.

"No," I said.

"Good, open your mouth. Wider, wider, wider, you silly man." Then he told me to close my mouth saying I looked stupid and he stood there with the rotten tooth in his pliers! I have had teeth out since then and, to be honest, this really was a painless extraction in comparison.

CHAPTER TWENTY

EAR EAR!

My trauma didn't end there. After our leave we were given another medical, to assess our fitness I presume.

I had been vaccinated against small pox in Glasgow before my call up. This was in October and now in November the medical officer wanted to do it again, despite the fact that I showed him a certificate proving I'd had it done already.

"You don't tell me what to do lad," he said, and jab went the needle.

Things went from bad to worse. I was directed to a side room and told to wait there in the freezing cold dressed only in trousers and singlet. I waited for ages in the cold. Eventually this MO appeared with his orderly, who was carrying a kidney tray and a huge syringe!

"Let's syringe your ears then," said the MO.

"No thanks, they don't need done," I said.

He said nothing, just gave me a look that said - don't waste my time arguing.

The water-loaded syringe was inserted in my left ear and battle commenced. All of a sudden there was a loud cracking sound and water poured down my nose into my mouth.
"Good, good," said the MO. "Get your clothes back on and wait there," he said, not bothering with the other ear.

Eventually I was taken into another room and confronted by three officers. The eldest of the three said to me, "We take a dim view of people damaging their ears to avoid National Service." I assured him and the others that this was not true. By this time I was in agony. "Very well," he said. "We will overlook it this time, off you go."

I was in pain for a week with no treatment and I certainly was not ever going back to see that MO if I could help it.

Years later in 1976 I had an ear infection and went to see my doctor. He surprised me by saying, "When did you burst your ear drum?" I had to plead ignorance and then I suddenly remembered the incident in the RAF, which had left me deaf in one ear and all these years I wasn't aware of it. However, some years later I was able to pursue a claim against the War Pensions and prove my case. I got a one-off payment, but no pension. Oh well, something was better than nothing I suppose.

CHAPTER TWENTY-ONE

HOME ON THE RANGE

Our weapons training was stepped up and the P.E. sessions increased. The idea of this was to get us ready for the assault course at the end of our training. We were told that if we did not complete this by the prescribed time or if we got ourselves or our kit dirty, we would have to do it all again. Have you seen the assault course?

After ensuring we were familiar with the weapons to hand, we were deemed fit to visit the rifle range and actually fire them. The weapons being the .303 rifle, Bren gun and the notorious Sten gun.

We were driven to the rifle range and issued with rounds of live ammunition - clips of bullets for the rifles and magazines for the Bren guns. We never got to use the Sten gun. You had to be in the prone position, listen to the instructions and fire at targets about 100/150 yards away. We were being supervised by several sergeants, corporals and one very highly strung young officer. We were told that if we did not get the required number of hits on the targets we would be held back and have to do it all again before we were "passed out." This really cheered us up, especially me as my Dad was a marksman during the First World War and had also been in the Machine Gun Corp so was pretty handy with weapons. Would I take after him? Perhaps not. We will see.

CHAPTER TWENTY-TWO

YOU'RE A BLOODY MURDERER!

Before we were allowed to fire a rifle we had to carry out the proper drill - tuck the butt of the rifle well into your shoulder, line up the sights and take aim. First, pressure on the trigger, put a bullet up the spout. Squeeze gently and fire.

Everybody satisfied that we all knew what we were doing, we were allowed to load the rifle and fire in our own time. You are well advised to tuck the rifle well in. Nothing prepares you for the kick back when the rifle fires. There was slight recoil from those .22 rifles at the fair ground, but this was something else and the noise was deafening.

My hands were quite steady, but my eyes were streaming with water. I could just about see the target. I got off a couple of rounds. Each time you hit or missed the target a flag would point out where people had scored or not. I didn't fancy being one of the people doing this and you will find out why!

The officer I mentioned was strutting up and down, taking in what was going on. He stopped beside me and said, "I know what you're doing wrong. You are breathing out before you pull the trigger, causing the rifle to lower the front of the sight. I will talk you through the drill again and see if we can get it right." Assuming the rifle was empty, we got to the part where he said, "Hold your breath, squeeze, squeeze again and fire," which I did. By this time the rest of the flight were collecting their targets. When my rifle went off, about eight or nine airmen hit the deck in front of the targets. The officer went mental, shouting, "You bloody murderer, you could have killed somebody!" I was terror-struck and almost passed out! The relief when I saw everyone get to their feet was palpable.

Strangely no action was taken against me. I think perhaps he felt as much, if not more, to blame as me.

I was allowed to carry on and whilst my score wasn't brilliant, it must have been enough to pass.

This was an experience I would never want to repeat and even now thinking about it, it gives me the shivers.

I never fired a weapon in anger and I don't know how I would have coped faced with trying to kill somebody. It was bad enough doing mock bayonet practice, running screaming and sticking a bayonet into a straw dummy, but to do it to a real person? Mind, you, we were still being told nearly every day: "Kill or be killed. It's him or you," so who knows?

On a lighter note, as I've said, the weather was very cold and the billet was not that warm. Corporal Jones was entertaining another corporal in his room at the end of the billet. One of the lads knocked on his door and remarked how cold it was. "No problem," said Corporal Jones. "Take Reilly with you, go down to the boiler room and bring back two buckets of steam."

We did as ordered, only my partner said to me, "I've got a better idea." When we got to the boiler room we borrowed a wheelbarrow and wheeled it back to the billet.

We knocked on the corporal's door and said, "We've got you a barrow full of steam too, Corporal. Where do you want it?" Fair does, he and his colleague took it in good humour.

CHAPTER TWENTY-THREE

WHERE WOULD YOU LIKE TO BE POSTED?

We were nearing the end of our time at dear old Gredon Hill, only the assault course and passing out parade to come.

With this in mind we were interviewed as to where our permanent postings would be. I was interviewed by a kindly grey haired old officer. A father figure; quite unlike anything we had been used to. He asked me what I would like to do. Get out of here as soon as possible, I thought.

He said that if I were to sign on for seven years they could offer me a choice of trades.

After what we had been through I thought, Seven years! No way, José! Then he asked me where I was from. "Glasgow, Sir," I told him.

He said there was an RAF base there and would I like to be posted there.

"I wouldn't mind Sir, that would be nice," said I. When my posting finally came through it would be to RAF 16 MU Stafford. Who said that the RAF didn't have a sense of humour? Glasgow – Stafford, only about 250 miles difference.

CHAPTER TWENTY-FOUR

THE ASSAULT COURSE

On the day we tackled the assault course the snow had almost gone, but had left the ground heavy and muddy. We were dressed in full kit, carrying our rifles with five rounds of blank ammunition (for obvious reasons).

We set off at intervals and had to negotiate various obstacles over the course. I suppose this is where the build-up of fitness would count.

The first obstacle was the rope wall, up and over. Next a bridge wall, followed by an open ditch filled with water, then down a hollow in the ground with a huge log covering it and you had to crawl under and out the other side of it.

At each obstacle there was a corporal of the RAF regiment. At the hollow there was a large black officer and, yes, he did have an American accent. The lad in front of me was, shall we say, quite heavily built, especially around the rear quarters. He slid under the log and instead of coming out the other side he got well and truly stuck!

"I'm stuck Corporal," he said, rather tearfully.

The following response from the corporal is ad verbatim. "You done stuck man?"

"Yes Corporal."

"I'll get you out there man." I thought he would try and pull the lad out. Instead he placed his rifle about six inches away from his rear end and fired! The lad shot out like a bullet out of a gun and was last seen fleeing in terror over the rest of the course.

At certain points of the assault course you had to fire at five targets and bayonet a dummy. All pretty straightforward you would say! The last obstacle was a piece of high ground which you had to run at and jump down. To my great surprise it was higher up than I thought.

I took off, flew through the air and landed on all fours on the muddy ground (we were wearing our denim work overalls or my uniform would have been covered in mud). However, upon landing, my rifle got stuck in the ground and I spent the last hundred yards of the course trying to pick the mud out of the barrel with my little finger. Remember, we were told if we got our rifles dirty we had to do the whole course again. Luckily the rifle looked clean apart from the mud at the end of the barrel and I got away with it.

CHAPTER TWENTY-FIVE

THE PASSING OUT PARADE

This was the final instalment of all the bull-shit, hard graft and discipline. Today we would parade before the top brass and compete for the trophy for best Flight.

Uniforms pressed, button and badges polished, webbing freshly blancoed. Thankfully no packs to worry about today. Oh, and boots, with the toe caps gleaming. It felt good to see the turnout of all the lads.

We were marched on to the sacred Parade Square where we were joined by an RAF band. We were inspected by the AOC and then marched past the saluting base. With the order, "Eyes right!" and, "Eyes front!" when we had passed the DIAS, the cup was then presented to the best flight (ours) and the best airman (not me). We were then lined up and had a photograph taken. There were a few parents there and they were all proud of their sons. They didn't know that we had been told we might be going to Korea. You may think of the RAF in terms of planes, but they had their own fighting force, the RAF regiment, who guarded air bases and other units, and ordinary airmen like ourselves were expected to turn soldier if needs be. Why else all that training?

I forgot one little blip before the parade. One bright spark had hidden my rifle and I panicked. You might as well go out naked on parade as go without a rifle! The culprit owned up at the last minute. He had hidden it under a mattress.

All that remained was for us to return said rifles to the armoury and our bedding to the stores and we would be free - for now anyway.

I suppose it was sad to think you would probably never see blokes you shared all that time with again.

People from all over England with their different outlooks and accents, some who had the nerve to tell me, "You don't half talk funny, Jock!" This would carry on into my working life, but I just thought it funny and took no offence, still do!

I regret that during my time at Hereford I didn't see much of the countryside. We did visit the place a couple of times and saw the cathedral and the food market. There seemed to be a lot of seed merchants and, of course, the famous football team, the FA Cup Giant Killers, but that would be years later. It would also be years later that I discovered what beautiful countryside there was. Of course, at the time, we were all too tired to appreciate our surroundings.

It had snowed again quite heavily. A coach had been hired to take us northerners home. How much it cost or who organised it I do not remember. I do know it was one of the most horrendous journeys I have ever been on though! It was bitter cold and the heating failed not long after we left. I think we picked other people up on the way.

What I do remember very well was a stop at the Jungle Café on the Shap Fell on the old A6 road. It's long gone now, replaced by modern service stations who don't provide steaming mugs of tea and sizzling sausage rolls, baps (or whatever people called them), all to be obtained for a few pence in those days. Being a transport café their prices were always cheaper. Rough and ready, but very welcoming on nights like that. I also remember the car park was like a skating rink and some clown came running in shouting that the bus was leaving, making people run outside in a panic. This produced a scene out of a comedy film with people sliding about all over the place and packets of crisps and bottles of pop flying everywhere, some never to be seen again!

The snow was still falling and, to add insult to injury, the driver told us we would all have to get out and push to give the wheels traction. I kid you not! I still think it was a wind up.

It must have cheered the driver up, the sight of forty odd blokes trying to push a bloody big coach!

Eventually we got going again, soaked, chilled and cheesed off. We stopped off in Carlisle at about midnight. Of course everywhere was closed. Then someone said he had found a hotel that was open (probably the same clown who told us the coach was leaving). We all piled off the coach and went downstairs to the basement to be met by the sight of all these old dossers and drunks lying around. It was what was known as a motel for the homeless and down and outs. No joy there then. All in all, the nightmare journey took over sixteen hours and I was more than glad to see old Glasgow again!

CHAPTER TWENTY-SIX

RAF 16 MU STAFFORD

I got confirmation of my posting to 16 MU, or 16th Maintenance Unit to give it its proper title, along with the usual travel warrant. And so another journey was about to begin.

I caught the London train timed to arrive in Stafford the following morning at about 06:00 hours. There would be no welcoming committee and I would have to find my own way to camp, courtesy of a Midland red double decker bus. The only way to travel, what!

I arrived on a cold, damp miserable morning. I was soon to find out that dampness was a feature of the area. It did nothing to cheer me up. Once again I hadn't got a clue what awaited me. As it turned out, it wasn't at all bad. I would spend the next eighteen months in the company of a great bunch of lads. Looked after by Warrant Officer Appleton and Flight Sergeant Scorgie, both regulars and both decent sorts, what!

My official title would be Admins Assistant, in other words, general dogsbody! But, as I said, it turned out not bad at all.

After breakfast on the first day I reported to the orderly room and was told that transport would take me to 3 Site, which was a couple of miles away from the main camp. This turned out to be a bonus. Out of sight, out of mind! By and large we were left alone to get on with it and only one SP (Special Policeman) to contend with, unlike the main camp which had a fair few of them, whose whole purpose in life was to upset everybody and anybody. I reported to the AIS Section, otherwise known as the Aeronautical Inspection Service. Quite a mouthful isn't it!

CHAPTER TWENTY-SEVEN

AIS

I was interviewed by Warrant Officer Appleton. The message was: "Keep your head down, your nose clean, meet your quotas every week and your time with us will be enjoyable." After Padgate and Hereford this seemed to be good to be true!

Our duties comprised of inspecting the various components of the Rebecca Radar Scanner. The largest of these was the cathode ray tube as used in televisions. I remember this well because the store men had a nasty habit of dropping them from a great height, creating an almighty bang as they imploded, making you jump about ten foot in the air whilst minding your own business. Each time you visited the stores you had to have your wits about you.

We had to test resistors and capacitors and valves using a mega. This was a device with a live and neutral terminal fitted with crocodile clips. Once you had the part wired up you cranked a handle and took a reading off the dial and passed or failed the part according to the reading.

We had two Welsh men in the group, 'Taffy' Hughes, a real live wire (get it), who used to crack us up with his singing, especially when we got him to sing all the latest hits in Welsh. Whoever said Welsh men could sing hadn't met Mr Hughes; Taffy that is, not Tom. The other one was Roberts. I swear he had been bitten by the tsetse fly. No matter what time of day it was he looked half dead.

Flight Sergeant Scorgie had been wounded during the war and, four years later, he was still having pieces of gun turret removed from his eyes. As a result he had poor vision - so he said.

We all played tricks on each other, like cranking up the mega, touching the terminal and then touching the lad next to you, who would then get a mild shock.

However, some of the capacitors had a high voltage and could give you a nasty bite! One day, Chiefy had had enough of Roberts and decided, in his own words, to, "wake the bastard up." He charged up a 4,000 volt one and, turning to Roberts, said, "Would you mind reading the serial number of this for me. I can't work it out." Knowing that his sight was poor, Roberts obliged. Chiefy handed it to him so that he had no option but to grip it by the end wires (if you picked it up by the body you didn't get a shock!).

One minute Roberts was sat at the bench, the next minute he was flying through the air and landed on his back in the corner of the room. His face was ashen grey. Well, more grey then usual! We all thought, "My God, he's killed him!" as Roberts lay there motionless. Mind you, as this was his natural state, it was hard to tell. All I know is it was the fastest he had moved to date! Roberts recovered and I would like to say that he moved faster after his shock, but he didn't and I don't think he ever would.

CHAPTER TWENTY-EIGHT

ALONG CAME A SPIDER

Most of the kit we had to inspect came from overseas; places like Malaysia, Singapore, etc. The lads over there thought it was hilarious to put various insects, small lizards and frogs inside the packing, most of which were dead before we opened the crates, ripped the wax covering off the sets, took the back off and began to test them.

One day there was a faint scratching noise coming from the crate. I opened the crate in the prescribed manner - small crowbar, Airman for the use of, and stripped the wax covering off. As I did this the scratching got louder. I removed the back and out shot this enormous spider, which proceeded to gallop down the bench. I have never seen a room empty so quickly, grown men panicking to get out of the door.

Taffy Hughes, being a bit braver than the rest of us, picked up a shovel and chased it along the floor. He walloped it at least six times before it gave up the ghost. These were bold lads who would be prepared to kill or be killed, scared to death by a spider! Trust me, if you had seen it you would have been too! Writing this now I have got goose pimples. It turns out that it was a bird-eating spider, which, whilst not venomous, could give you a nasty bite (according to my mother, so could an elephant. Don't ask!)

CHAPTER TWENTY-NINE

WHERE'S THE FIRE?

Both Scorgie and Appleton had a wicked sense of humour, but could still maintain discipline when required. The summer of '51 was quite a good one and, during the lunch breaks, we used to go up on the roof to sunbathe. They both knew this, but weren't bothered about it (Health and Safety!).

One really hot day we were sunbathing as usual, some of us in the buff, when we heard the fire bell ringing. This was not unusual as there were regulation fire drills from time to time so we stayed where we were.

Looking down we saw Flight Sergeant Scorgie, Appleton and an officer from another section running the fire cart, which was just that, a two wheeled cart with a very large hose which you attached to a fire hydrant. The fact that they all knew where we were and yet hadn't ordered us down never struck us as being strange. It never registered with us at the time, but we soon found out why. Shouting, "Fire, fire!" and laughing like maniacs, they turned on the hose and proceeded to drown us with a deluge of water. Knowing full well we shouldn't have been on the roof all we could do was lie there and take it on the chin - and everywhere else! Those of us without clothes came off the best. The others were a bedraggled lot, but we all soon dried off in the heat and had a good laugh about it.

CHAPTER THIRTY

FOOTBALL

I was minding my own business one day when I was called to the WO's office. "Sit down, Reilly," he said. I wondered what was coming next. He said that the Intersectional Cup was coming up and he had decided to enter a team this year. A team? What, with seven people, one of whom had sleeping sickness and two old men - well to me they were. "As you are the only Scotsman on the site you can be captain and pick the team!" What an honour, more like a poisoned chalice. Anyway, anything for a laugh.

We scraped together a team using lads from the Signals Section. There were no substitutes in those days so we had just the bare bones of a team, eleven men. We were drawn against a team of clerks from 3 Site. Included in their team was a Warrant Officer, Ward by name, who, in later days, would give us great excitement on his part, rather unwittingly. He had a rather endearing nickname of Chunky because of his build. His arse was too near the ground, as they say!

We were allowed Wednesday afternoons off for sport, so it was we played our first cup tie. I for one thought it would also be our last. We had at least sorted out who would play where, except for Brian Taylor, a 6' 2" giant with hands like shovels. It took a lot of persuasion to convince him that, although he had played little football and never in goal, he looked the part of a fierce goalie. I had played youth football in Glasgow as a forward, but decided to play in defence in effort to keep the score down. It was a very scrappy game and the other side weren't much better than us.

Wardie was flying around, kicking anything that got in his way. After a while, I'd had enough and shouted, "Get stuck into it, Chunky." He looked surprised and it was obvious that he was not aware of his nickname or why people followed up Chunky with "the man with the pineapple balls!"

He came running over and grabbed me by the jersey. "Chunky! Where did that come from," he screamed.

Red in the face, I said, "It's meant as a compliment, Sir, because of your strong chunky frame." If only he knew the rest of it! The referee told us to behave and cut out the language, this being addressed to everyone. Later we would find out that he was in fact a Catholic priest when we got dressed after the match! Red faced or what!

We managed, by good luck rather than anything else, to win the match and progress to the second round much to the disgust of Warrant Officer Ward, but to the delight of our own Mr Appleton.

We met the Catering Section, who, along with the Transport Section, were favourites to win the cup. The match was played on one of the main pitches at the main camp. Before being called up I had only ever played on cinder pitches so it was a novelty to play on grass with good nets, avoiding disputes as to whether a goal had been scored or not. Even in those days there were some short-sighted referees around in the youth club league! It was a joy to play on grass. If you went down on a cinder pitch your knees and elbows were pitted with bits of ash and it was a very, very painful experience having them removed, mostly by my Dad using a household scrubbing brush, nothing as refined as a nail brush. "You have got to be cruel to be kind," was his motto!

I digress! So, back to the match and I will hand you over to your commentator for the day, me! The pitch was roped off and I was surprised to see quite a large crowd assembled to witness the battle between David and Goliath! I told the lads, based on the fact that the other side were older than us and had a few drinkers in their ranks, "I don't want to see any of you in their half of the pitch for the first twenty minutes," hoping that they would tire themselves out and thus keep the score down and avoid total humiliation on our part. This tactic worked quite well. They battered us with everything, but couldn't score. The sight of "Big Brian" in goal didn't help them and, psychologically was putting them off.

If only they had known how terrified he was! We got to half time with the score 0-0.

During half time I told Brian that when he got the chance, to kick the ball into the other team's half and I would run on to it (a common tactic in those days). He didn't have many chances to do this as we were still under siege. However, with about ten minutes to go, he got the ball and saw me waving and shouting at him to boot it up the pitch. I wasn't a great footballer, but I could run fast. This took the other side by surprise and, as they were all in our half of the park, when I got the ball, off I went towards their goal. I could hear pounding boots behind me and, as I got closer, heavy breathing. The goalie didn't move and I was just about to aim for goal when my legs were chopped at the knees and down I went. Penalty! But would the ref give it? Yes he would. Brave man! I placed the ball on the spot (no one else volunteered). Suddenly this figure appeared beside me. It was a corporal from the cook house.

"If you score this, Lofty, you'll never eat again at the camp."

The referee warned him off. I toe-ended the ball past the keeper and looked forward to eating in the NAAFI for the rest of my time (or food parcels from Scotland!). I went to dinner that evening. The corporal was there, but made no comment and I breathed a sigh of relief.

We had pulled off a miracle and won 1-0. WO Appleton was a very happy man. Our joy didn't last long (a week) and we were well beaten in the next round, but at least we had knocked out one of the favourites and we were very popular with the Transport lads, who went on to win the cup.

Football got me into a little spot of bother later on. A lad called Bobby Gilroy had signed '5' forms for Celtic and was a pretty useful player, but not, it seemed, good enough to play for the Station team.

All blue-eyed boys to the last man, players like Brian Pilkington (who went on to play for Burnley and was a youth international for England) who, when we were having a knockabout and I tackled him, shouted, "You Jocks are all mad," and left the pitch in a huff! As Corporal Jones said, "They don't like it up 'em!"

Anyway, Brian played for an amateur team in a village just outside Stafford. The teams got ready in the local pub and when you opened the French doors at the rear of the pub you were straight on to the pitch. Very picturesque. Bobby asked me to go with him one Saturday. The "Brock" were playing the Royal Engineers in a cup tie. Whilst I was waiting for the game to start, the secretary asked me, "Do you kick a ball?"

I said I had been known to and he asked me if I would like a game, saying they were one man short and that Bobby said I might play. I said I would, but had no kit with me.

"No problem," he said, and kitted me out. We lost 7-3 and I have never been kicked or abused so many times on a football field as I was that day.

I got dressed after the game and, as I put my shoes on I felt something in the toe of one of them. I put my hand in and pulled out two bank notes, in total £1.10 shillings (£1.50). I called out, "Somebody has dropped some money."

"Don't be an idiot, that's what we get for playing," Bobby said. "Put it in your pocket."

I played a couple more matches until the injured lad was fit again. I enjoyed the money until one morning Mr Appleton said, "The CO wants to see you in his office at 10:00 hours tomorrow. What have you been up to?"

"Nothing I can think of!" I said. I duly presented myself at Headquarters the next day and guess who was sat outside the CO's office? None other than B. Gilroy Esq.! "What are you doing here?" I asked. He said likewise. We were shown into Wing Commander Budd's office and told to sit down.

"Do you two play football?" he asked.

"Yes Sir," I said, thinking it was hardly likely he was interviewing us for the station team.

"Do you play for Brock United?" he asked. We said yes, although in my case, only a couple of times, whilst Bobby played on a regular basis. "Do you realise it against King's Regulations to do any job for money outside the Air Force?" he asked.

"Oh, yes, Sir," we lied! I didn't know we had committed a crime.

"You play on a Saturday and don't get any money?"

"No, Sir," we chorused.

"I see, off you go then." We had just reached the door when he said, "Come back you two. You play for nothing every week?"

"Oh, yes, Sir," said we in unison. Oh no, we've been caught lying to the CO! I thought.

"Well," he said. "In my opinion you're a couple of bloody idiots! Off you go."

We never found out who had grassed on us. As far as I know, we didn't have any enemies. Anyway, we now had the CO's blessing, or at least a blind eye to the matter!

Football was also to be the cause of my only court appearance and one I did not enjoy. We used to go and see Wolves on a Saturday (that's when they had a team) when we could. We went to Stafford Station, Gilroy and I, to get the train to Wolverhampton. When we got to the ticket office one day there was a queue. We had cut it a bit neat and the train was standing at the platform. Bobby asked the people in front if we could go before them and they all said yes, except for a well-dressed gent at the front. Bobby explained to him that our train was ready to leave and asked him if he would let us go before him.

"No!" was the blunt reply. Before I realised what was happening, Bobby jumped the barrier and got on the train. Like an idiot I followed him, a decision I would come to regret. We discussed the 'nice mannered gent' and thought it would be okay to pay at the other end. When we got off the train however, we were met by two of the Railway Police's finest.

"We have reason to believe you have travelled without a valid ticket and haven't paid the appropriate fare," they told us. We said that wasn't a problem as we had the money in our hands to pay. This did not wash with our two friends and they took us to their office, took our details and then asked us where we were going.

"To the match," we said. They kept us in until half time, the reason being they had to confirm our details. We were charged with non fare paying and the summons arrived about a month later. I had to explain to Mr Appleton what had taken place. He arranged for us to have an officer with us to help state our case. We appeared before the beaks at Stafford Court. After listening to our tale they retired to consider their verdict. It didn't take long.

The verdict was: "Guilty." The summing up stunned us. "We have had enough of you yobs from Glasgow causing trouble in our town," they said. Causing trouble? Two unpaid fares was causing trouble? The young officer with us told the magistrates that we were not troublemakers. Despite this we were fined £2.10 shillings each (£2.50) with no time to pay. The officer said that he would take care of the fines and it would be deducted from our pay. It never was and I can only surmise he paid them from his own pocket. Not an experience I would wish to repeat any time soon!

CHAPTER THIRTY-ONE

COLD RUNNING WATER

Our billet building was not very salubrious. In the winter, Staffordshire was very damp and, as a result, the roof and walls of the billet ran with water. In the morning the bedding was always damp. I wonder how many people ended up with arthritis living in such damp conditions. Add to those conditions forty-two men, some of whom enjoyed a good drink, and you can imagine the aromas wafting round the billet!

Then there were the people who had the annoying habit of coming in at all hours and waking us up. One in particular, a little Welsh G.I.T who would shake you awake with the immortal words, "Would you like to buy a battleship?" I had had enough of him and decided to 'sort him out'. Pretending to be asleep one night, I heard him come in falling over beds and, as usual, waking everyone up. He came up to my bed assuming that I was the only one asleep. "Do you want to buy a battleship, Jock?" he said. I uncoiled my fist from beneath the blankets and socked him in the mouth! Strangely enough we never heard him again. (How dare he call me Jock, the Taffy!)

CHAPTER THIRTY-TWO

AT LAST, A TASTE OF LUXURY

I was fortunate enough to have made good friends with a lad called Jimmy Lynagh, a fellow Glaswegian who had the same wacky sense of humour as me. He was a driver in the Transport Section and had just moved into the newly built barrack blocks. They had individual rooms and a four-berth room at the end of each corridor. They also had shower rooms and pristine toilets. Each room had a single bed complete with one piece mattress and a bed lamp above the bed, a double wardrobe and under floor heating, along with a window that opened. No running water down the walls, in other words, sheer luxury!

I said to Jimmy that I felt really envious of his situation. He said I should apply for one of the rooms, but I told him I didn't think I had a chance as I hadn't really "got some in." There were people who had been in the RAF since Pontius was a pilot and Nero was a fire picket, so what chance did I have?

I did apply however and, to my delight, I was allocated a single room with all mod cons. I was next door to the four-berth room and across the corridor was Paddy Lynch. He was a real loner. When he had leave he would spend it drinking in his room and would never come out of it. I came back off leave one time and looked in on him. There was no sign of him. I thought he must have gone home at last. I was about to leave when I heard this snoring coming from under his bed. There was Paddy, fully dressed, sound asleep under the bed! I had some difficulty waking him up, but he eventually came to. He remembered finishing a bottle of gin (his favourite tipple) and then nothing after that. He must have been there for at least a day! The thing about Paddy was that no matter how drunk he got, he never seemed to suffer any ill-effects. I supposed his lifestyle would catch up with him some day.

In the four-berth room there were two real characters, one from Liverpool and one from London, an unlikely combination, but they got on like a house on fire. 'Scouse' was 6' 2," whilst the other one was small in comparison. They had us in stitches with their rendition of 'A Policeman's Lot is Not a Happy One,' and other Gilbert and Sullivan tunes. The laugh was that Scouse sang in a deep voice and his pal sang in a high voice. Their version of Laurel and Hardy's 'Blue Ridge Mountains of Virginia' had us all in tears. They also led the singing of the usual songs (Airmen for the use of), which I'm afraid I can't repeat in print, not even the milder ones!

CHAPTER THIRTY-THREE

DO YOU COME FROM A FILTHY HOME?

We had kit inspections now and then, which surprised me. I thought I was done with all that! They were held on a Saturday morning when everyone was looking forward to a lie-in in their "stinking pits," as they were so charmingly described. I can only imagine the saying arose from the result of forty plus bodies living together in an enclosed space with all the attendant smells and aromas that went with those conditions. Thankfully I was away from all that now, and the cold running water.

As usual, for kit inspection, you had to lay your kit out in the prescribed order, even to the bar of soap (to prove you washed no doubt). Being a smart arse, I thought it would lighten the mood if I put my number 3130146 on the soap so, taking a darning needle from my 'housewife' (a sewing kit), I etched the number on the soap and thought no more of it.

The Inspecting Officer came in with a Flight Sergeant, complete with notebook for the use of taking naughty airmen's names. He ran his eye over the room and seemed happy until he saw the number on the soap. "Are you taking the piss, lad?"

"No Sir, it's my soap." Things went downhill from there. He picked up my mug, which had a small chip in it.

"Do you live in a pigsty at home?" he said. "Using a germ riddled mug to drink from?" With that he dropped the mug on the floor and, of course, it smashed. At 1/6 (7 ½ pence) for a replacement, I was not happy. He then took his hand across the top of the door and it was filthy. I had never even thought about the top of the door! Everywhere else was spotless. "Just as I thought - a pigsty," he said.

If only he had known how fussy my mother was about housework. She could spot a speck of dust at ten paces! "Take this man's name, Sergeant!" Strangely I never heard any more about it, but to this day I regularly dust the tops of doors at home. If my time in the RAF taught me nothing else, it taught me this!

Life continued apace. I had a nice billet, good company and a cushy job. What more could one ask for? Of course my life wasn't my own for the next eighteen months and I missed civvy street. I must also confess to a certain amount of boredom and in Stafford there was not a lot to do. However, we did have a camp cinema and theatre which, from time to time, showed some decent films and put on shows performed by the airmen themselves.

CHAPTER THIRTY-FOUR

THE RAF GOT TALENT!

Jimmy and I went to one of the shows at the theatre. There was a lad who mimed to records, who was very good. This was long before today, where it is now the norm for performers to mime to their latest hit, performers who, in the main, cannot sing! This fellow was so good it was hard to tell he was not actually singing. He did Bing Crosby, Al Johnson, Dean Martin as well as a few comic songs and went down very well with what could be a critical audience who had no hang ups at letting performers know if they thought they were rubbish!

We had a big lad in our block by the name of John Seed and, yes, he was a real life farmer's boy with a great Norfolk accent, me dear! John had a sense of humour. The only trouble was he was always a good few minutes behind everyone else at getting the joke or the punch line. This caused great hilarity. He would sit there poker-faced and appear not to get it. Suddenly, when everyone else had stopped laughing, John would start, "Ha, ha," slowly, then build up to a crescendo of, "Ha, ha, ha," and set us all off again. He also had a habit of laughing in the wrong place sometimes. It was well worth the shilling (5 pence) we paid to hear John getting revved up!

CHAPTER THIRTY-FIVE

OSCAR

Another act was a lad with 'Oscar, the performing flea'. He produced a matchbox and took out Oscar. He then announced that Oscar would perform a somersault. He asked for a drum roll, and threw Oscar up into the air. Then, by a series of appropriate head movements, he indicated that Oscar was turning over. He then caught him on the back of his hand.

"Oscar will now perform a double somersault." Again, drum roll, and, with two nods of his head, Oscar had completed the double. Now, with a solemn face: "Ladies and gentlemen, this trick has never been done by any flea in the world and I would ask for complete silence whilst Oscar attempts this. Can I have a drum roll please?" The drummer obliges and, after a few false starts, Oscar is off – one, two, three somersaults and then Oscar disappears, much to the dismay of his trainer and to the amusement of the audience. The trainer crawls around the stage calling for Oscar, but no joy. Suddenly he gets down from the stage and starts searching through the hair of one of the officers on the front row. "Ah, Oscar," he says, picking him out of the officer's hair, and putting him back in his matchbox, much to our amusement.

"Ladies and gentlemen, you may have noticed that Oscar didn't quite manage the triple, so we will try again." There followed the same routine, drum roll, Oscar up in the air, this time however he came straight back down with not even one somersault! Baffled, the young lad picked up Oscar, examined him and then, looking straight at the officer, said: "This is not Oscar!" Cue curtains and then spotlight on one red-faced officer and laughter all around.

CHAPTER THIRTY-SIX

IT'S A KNOCKOUT

No, not the famous one with Stuart Hall and Eddy Waring! This was an exhibition match between two of the station boxing teams, which took place on the same programme as Oscar and others. It was supposed to be an exhibition of the noble art between two fighters, one English and one Scottish.

The Scotsman was from Glasgow and considered himself a hard man. Quite frankly, both men were rubbish and the crowd let them know it! The Scotsman took exception to one of the officers who had been knocking him and exchanged a few words with him between rounds. The officer wouldn't give up and continued to abuse him. Suddenly, Jock jumped over the ropes, the only action we had seen from him all night, and before anyone could stop him, he floored the officer with one punch. He was promptly hurried away and we didn't see him for a while after that.

He obviously hadn't learned his lesson because some time later Jimmy and I were at the Town Hall Saturday night dinner dance. There was an upstairs balcony café and everyone was dancing away when, out of the blue, tables and chairs came flying down from the café and there was the bold lad doing the hurling! It appeared to have started over a girl he fancied, but who was already taken. This hadn't stopped Jock and, when her partner complained, Jock went berserk. It is a wonder people down below were not injured. The police were called and Jock was led away. We never did see him again after that!

CHAPTER THIRTY-SEVEN

YOU'VE BEEN CONNED

We all went to the Town Hall a few times as well as going to Hanley, Stoke-on-Trent, where they had the dance band half way up the wall! The first time we went I could hear the music, but I couldn't see any band until I looked up and saw them suspended in mid-air. More about Hanley later, and Ginger and his motorbike.

One Saturday we went dancing at the Town Hall. Half way through the evening, Jimmy came up to me and said: "I've got us fixed up with a couple of nurses. They work at St George's Hospital and have invited us to a dance there next week." At the end of the night they told us that they would meet us at the Hospital at about 8.00 pm.

We set off to get to the hospital on the bus. It dropped us off at the bottom of a long drive. A large notice said 'St George's Hospital,' but the bottom half of the notice was covered by bushes so we couldn't see the rest of it. We were soon to find out!

We were confronted by two large wooden doors and a notice saying: 'Please ring the bell.' This we did and heard the door being unlocked. We were greeted by the matron. "Welcome to St George's. Are you here for the dance?"

"Yes," said we.

"I'm so glad to see you. We invite you RAF lads every month, but nobody ever comes," she said.

The matron took us through to the hall. At this point we couldn't see our two nurses. Looking around we could see what the missing words on that board were. We were in the local loony bin! Yes it was a dance all right, but not as we know it! To say it was old fashioned is an understatement, plus the looks we were getting because we were in uniform gave me the impression that the patients felt sorry for us, us thinking we were in the RAF! Some of them were whirling around like dervishes; others were pointing at us and laughing.

We sought out the matron and told her we had by invited by two of her nurses, but couldn't find them anywhere. She asked us to describe them, but from our description she didn't recognise them and they were certainly not amongst the nurses on duty that night. Then the penny dropped. We had well and truly been conned.

The following Saturday we were on Stafford Main Street and spotted the two nurses coming out of a shoe shop. When they saw us they burst out laughing and said, "Did you enjoy the dance?"

"Not much, we left after half an hour when we couldn't find you two," we said.

Turned out the two of them were sales girls in the shoe shop and had tried this trick a few times, but we were the only two mugs who had fallen for it. So far!

My other lasting memory of the Town Hall was coming out into a side lane and seeing a couple having sex while she ate cod and chips over his shoulder, ugh!

Talking about fish and chips, we used to visit the chippie before we got the bus back to camp. Jimmy used to drive the girl behind the counter mad. Every time she said: "What would you like, me duck," he would dive down under the counter pulling me with him and laughing like a maniac. The poor girl hadn't a clue what it was all about!

CHAPTER THIRTY-EIGHT

WARRANT OFFICER WARD

I have mentioned Wardie before and what a character he was. I'd like to take you through a few of his howlers.

The Warrant Officers had a mess meeting once a month. During one such meeting they were discussing improvements to the mess, after which they would have a vote as to which ones to adopt. One of the items suggested was chandeliers to brighten the place up! They took a vote on this and Mr Appleton, the Chairman, said, "Mr Ward, you haven't voted yes or no to the chandeliers."

Wardie replied, "I've nothing against chandeliers, but no-one can play them!" You couldn't make it up!

The lads in Wardie's office used to play him up something rotten. He would call out to them and they would ignore him completely. One day he lost it and shouted, "Why do you lot never hear me?"

One of the lads said, "It's the acoustics Sir, they are very bad in this office."

"Well get the bloody things changed then," he shouted and wondered why they all fell about laughing.

My own experience of him came when I was Duty Runner going between 3 site and the main camp on a bicycle. As I was going through the gate, Wardie, who was on the phone in his office opposite the Guard Room, opened a window and shouted, "Airman. Yes, you. Get off your bike and see if Corporal so and so is in the Guards Room."

I thought it was obvious, as he got no reply that he wasn't there (but this was Wardie!). However I went into the Guards Room and the phone was still ringing so I picked it up and said, "3 site Guards Room."

"Who is that?" asked Wardie, who could actually see me from the window!

"It's me Sir, you told me to answer the phone!"

"Is Corporal so and so there?" he asked.

"No Sir," I said.

"Well get off the bloody phone then!" he shouted.

CHAPTER THIRTY-NINE

THE MOCK BATTLE

We were told there was going to be a mock raid on 3 Site by the Army and it would last 24 hours. We were given our duties and told we would be on guard four hours on and two off. We were not told when the attack would take place, but there would be marshals observing things and deciding who had been killed, etc. There would be no ammo and you had to shout, "Bang," at the enemy! I am being serious.

Taylor and I patrolled one of the fences during the night and were scared rigid when we heard this noise echoing along the wire only to find out it was a cow rubbing its horns along the wire! After our first few hours we went to the Guards Room and had some tea. It was a bitter cold night and the tea was welcome. I asked the corporal where we would sleep. He laughed and pointed to the concrete floor. If anyone had told me I would sleep fully clothed on a concrete floor I would have dismissed it out of hand but, believe me, I was so tired I did just that.

The attack came at about 10:00 hours the next morning. A lorry drove up to the main gate, but the Special Police quickly closed and secured them.

The soldiers piled out of the lorry and started yelling and screaming on one side of the fence whilst we were on the other side. Both sides were shouting, "Bang," at each other and, despite the marshals saying, "You're dead," both sides refused to lie down and die. What a blooming shambles! The attack didn't last long. One of the soldiers threw a smoke grenade over the fence. Wardie, our hero, picked it up and attempted to throw it back. Instead it landed on top of the Headquarters building and exploded. The marshals decided that as the Headquarters had been destroyed it was game over and we were all captured (Wardie strikes again). God help us if it had been the real thing.

CHAPTER FORTY

LET YOUR BALLS DANGLE

The AOC (Air Officer Commander) was due to visit 16 MU for an inspection of the camp and the men and women. There were WAAFs on the base.

Mr Ward was in charge of keeping order among the assembled masses until the AOC arrived to inspect us. We were standing for ages and getting a bit restless and you could hear talking, which was not allowed. Wardie yelled at the top of his voice, "Quiet!" and the talking stopped, not for long though. "Silence!" he roared again. "Every time I open my mouth some damn fool speaks," he screamed, and wondered why there was an outbreak of laughter in the ranks. This caused his face to go purple with rage.

Then he came out with the absolute gem! Because we had been waiting a long time for the AOC, he said, "I don't want any of you fainting so here is a tip for you all. Relax your body if you feel faint, drop your arms by your sides, relax your knees . . ." and, best of all, "Let your balls dangle!" The image of all those WAAFs doing just that was too much to take. I know some of them did look a bit manly, but not to that extent. Poor old Wardie, he had done it again and shown himself up.

The AOC finally arrived and began his inspection. We had been warned to polish and press our uniforms and make sure our shoes were gleaming. The whole camp had gone bull-shit mad! Stones painted, grass cut and all the vehicles washed and polished. Even the menu in the mess was much improved from the usual. He walked up and down the ranks along with his entourage and, oh no, stopped in front of me.

It must be the Forage cap, I thought, sticking out a mile among all those berets. But it wasn't.

"I'm admiring your buttons and cap badge, lad. How did you get them so clean?" he asked.

I knew what he meant. Because the buttons have the Flying Eagle on them, the dirt lodged along the wings and beak. The cap badge had the same problem.

I told him my Dad was an old soldier and he had shown me on his tram driver uniform, which had brass buttons and his cap, which had a silver badge, how to clean off the dirt (which was a residue of Brasso really) with the point of a darning needle. Although they looked clean there was always this hint of dried Brasso around. The AOC was very impressed and said that he would remember this tip in future. To be passed on to his batman no doubt! I can't image him doing his own brasses.

I took some stick off the lads for this. "Reilly's the AOC's pet," they would say, but the novelty soon wore off. I still can't get those WAAFs out of my mind!

CHAPTER FORTY-ONE

THE MESS

I was not a big fan of our Force food. My mother had spoiled me for choice and if I didn't like something she would provide an alternative. There would only be two choices in the RAF – take it or leave it! After spending a few bob I couldn't afford in the NAAFI, I soon learned to eat or starve.

On night on the menu there was toad in the hole. I was not familiar with this and asked one of the lads what it was. "It's sausage in a Yorkshire pudding batter, Jock. It tastes okay." I decided to give it a go. I presented my plate and was given a dollop of batter and a ladle of peas (minus the Brasso). When I got back to the table and sat down (there were about twenty men to a table), I noticed something missing from my plate. Everyone had a sausage apart from me.

I went back to the server and said, very politely, "I haven't got a sausage with my dinner."

I was given a dirty look, pulled over the hot plate by my tie and told, "You had a bleeding sausage when you left here, now clear off!" So the sausage had vanished between the serving and the table. As the plate hadn't left my hand I knew it hadn't been stolen. So it remains a mystery to this day. First a broken plate at Padgate with sausage on it and now this! It gave everyone a good laugh though.

In fact we had quite a few laughs in the mess. When you were queuing up for your meals, if anyone jumped the queue the whole line would point at the offender and shout, "Queue!" until the Duty Sergeant would come along and make them go right to the back of the queue.

The other thing to cause me great embarrassment on a date after being demobbed was this. If anybody dropped a plate or a mug and it broke, all the idiots in the mess would cheer, leaving the culprit with a red face and a bill for a new mug or plate.

I took this girl to a posh restaurant in Glasgow for a meal and afterwards a cabaret. During the meal, a waiter came out of the kitchen and dropped about four plates, which of course all smashed on the floor. Like a complete idiot I jumped to my feet and cheered, only to be met by a stony silence. The girl looked at me as if I were mental, but seemed to accept my explanation it was an Air Force tradition and I had just got carried away (I probably should have been). Strangely enough I never saw her again. I wonder why?

The other entertainment my mate Jimmy and I had was outside the mess where there was a large tank filled with boiling water, the idea being that you swilled your knife, fork, spoon and your mug through the water to clean them. Jimmy, with his sense of humour, had discovered that if you waited long enough there would be a collision of mugs leaving people with just a handle each. This resulted in some bad language and sometimes fisticuffs, which we thought was hilarious. How sad were we? At 1/6 a mug, other people didn't find it funny as we were still only on 13 shillings a week.

CHAPTER FORTY-TWO

PURPLE TEA NOT RAIN

The other event that took place in the mess was the purple tea incident. The tea was normally strained through a muslin cloth before it went into a large tea urn. One night apparently there were no cloths to hand so the tea was strained through an RAF issue pullover. The result being that when the tea was dispensed from the urn it was purple, which amused us no end (I thought Brasso in the peas was bad enough!) The offending urn was removed and that was that, or so we thought. Someone had contacted the local paper and an article appeared a day later entitled, 'The case of the purple tea.' The CO was said to be furious and his face matched the colour of the tea! I don't know if the perpetrator ever owned up, but it gave us a laugh.

My own face was red a few weeks later when I read the menu and discovered there was no jam on the table (a rare treat). I spoke to the Duty Officer, who used to come round and say, "Any complaints?" and then glare at you as if to say - don't you dare complain!

"Yes Sir," I said that day. "I have a complaint. According to the menu, there should be jam on the table and there isn't." He marched me up to the serving hatch and demanded to know why there was no jam on the table.

"Because Sir," came the reply, "that's last week's menu, which hasn't been taken down yet. The new one is by the server."

I was given a lecture on how to read dates and told that I was lucky not to be put on a charge for wasting the CO's time. Hence the red face.

CHAPTER FORTY-THREE

THE NAAFI

Apart from the odd trip into Stafford for entertainment, it was not very exciting. Even the cinema closed at 9.30 pm and after that the place was like a ghost town. We did get excited one day though when an old lady stopped on a zebra crossing in front of a car transporter and caused uproar when all the cars on the transporter clanged together and the cars behind it had to stop suddenly. The old dear just carried on walking and disappeared into the Post Office unaware of the chaos she had caused.

Another time, Jimmy and I re-enacted a scene from the Marx Brothers film when they hail a taxi and say, "Take us to the Waldorf." All the time they are outside the Waldorf so it was in one door and out the other before the taxi driver could blink!

We did this on Stafford Main Street; we hailed the taxi, went in one door whilst calling out, "Take us to the Grapes Pub," which the taxi was already outside, and then jumped out the other door shouting, "That was quick!" The taxi driver followed us into the pub and was not a happy bunny to say the least. He couldn't see the funny side of it. Obviously not a Marx Brothers fan then!

The NAAFI was our other source of entertainment, such as it was. A snooker table, table tennis table and the usual cards, darts and dominoes, plus tea, coffee, beer and spirits, if you drank, which I didn't, and, of course, the good old NAAFI van used to come round the site every morning at about ten o'clock. For a few pence you could get a tea and a wad (cake). It took me a while to figure out why, when I was on leave, I was starving every morning at about ten o'clock. My mother used to say, "You can't be hungry; you've just had your breakfast." Then it sunk in. This was NAAFI van time and I'd got used to it, hence the hunger pangs at ten o'clock!

We were in the NAAFI one night and we were telling jokes and the usual tall stories (or "shooting the shit" as it was known). Jimmy told a joke about someone with a stutter, not politically correct these days is it? It was about a young officer taking Guard Duty for the first time with a bunch of raw recruits.

"If you hear someone approaching, you call out ffff . . . friend or fff . . . foe? If you get nnn . . . no answer, call again ffff . . . friend or fff . . . foe? If you get no answer the second time shshshsh . . . shoot ttt . . . to kkkk . . . kill. But wait a while as it mmmm . . . might be mmm . . . me!" After telling the joke, Jimmy went up to the counter and stuttered, "Tttt . . . two ttt . . . teas mm . . . miss."
The girl slapped him hard across the face and said, "Are you ttt . . . taking the pp . . . piss?" We all fell about laughing. This time the joke was on Jimmy!

Another time we were walking past the parade ground. This was sacred ground. You were not allowed to walk across it at any time other than when we were actually on parade. Jimmy was smoking and tossed his dog end on to the parade ground (shock, horror). He was spotted by an officer, who asked, "Airman, is that your cigarette?"

"Oh no, Sir," says Jimmy, "You have it; you saw it first!" Luckily for him he had met someone with the same daft sense of humour as him. Lucky Jimmy indeed.

I got another red face some time later. Wednesday afternoon was recreational day. I used to play badminton with another lad. One day I arrived early at the hanger that housed the badminton courts. There was a WAAF there dressed in P.E. kit.

After a few minutes she said, "My partner is a bit late."
"So is mine," I said.

She suggested we have a knock about until they both arrived. I played football, table tennis and badminton for the youth club and I considered myself to be quite a good player. We knocked the shuttlecock about then she said, "Let's have a proper game."

"Okay," I said, thinking it would be a shame to beat her! How wrong was I? She wiped the floor with me and by the time our partners arrived I was cream crackered. Her partner asked me if I had enjoyed the game.

Aye right, I thought, beaten by a woman!

"Do you know who you were playing?" No, I didn't. "She's the West of England champion." Cue red face and lesson learned. Don't take anything for granted in the future!

CHAPTER FORTY-FOUR

HITCH HIKING

As those of you who have done National Service will know, the pay was lousy. Even after eighteen months it was just about two pounds per week. All right, I know board and lodgings were free, so I suppose two quid seemed like a lot of money, but when it came to travel away from camp it would soon be eaten up. So it was decided we would hitch-hike!

Scouse said we should try and get to New Brighton using our thumbs. We got the bus (yes I know), four of us, to the outskirts of Stafford and so the adventure began.

I hadn't got a clue where New Brighton was, but Scouse said it was near Liverpool. We were only at the side of the road for a few minutes when a cattle truck pulled up.

"Where are you going, lads?" asked the driver.

"The other side of Liverpool," said Scouse.

"You'll be bloody lucky," said he and drove off laughing. Thanks a lot mate!

Every time a vehicle passed and didn't stop, Scouse gave it the two finger salute. We told him it was no way to win friends and influence people, but it didn't stop him! We had been there for quite a while and were beginning to think it wasn't such a good idea, although we had a 48-hour pass so we had time to get there and back. A large American car drove past and, as usual, Scouse gave it the two fingers. The car came to a stop, reversed back and, to our horror, an American Air Force officer stepped out. He eyed up our uniforms and asked us where we were going. We told him we were heading for Liverpool.

"Okay, jump in, I'm going that way," he said. Lucky or what? He chatted away to us and asked us where we were stationed and whether we were regulars.

"National Service," we explained. He asked us if we were hungry. Politely we said no.

"Well I am," he said, and pulled into a roadside café. "You're welcome to join me," he said. So we did. We had a meal and he insisted on paying. What a decent chap! The second American I had met and they were both decent fellows. He dropped us off by the docklands and we did a 'Freddie and the Dreamers,' catching the ferry across the Mersey. New Brighton had a bit of a beach and a fun-fair. We spent a few hours there then headed back.

If the journey there had been easy, the trip back was a nightmare. Liverpool was very busy and no-one stopped for us. We walked all the way from the city centre to the city boundary, a distance of seven miles I understand. A taxi pulled up and we said, "Sorry we didn't realise you were a taxi." The driver asked us where we were going. "Stafford," we said.

"I can take you to Knutsford where I live at no charge," he offered. Gratefully we piled into the taxi. He asked us about National Service and told us his son had just been called up and he and his wife were worried about him especially as the Korean War was still going on. I didn't tell him what we had been told about Korea and the others kept quiet. He dropped us off and it was getting quite late.

We saw a bread lorry coming and Scouse being Scouse started thumbing. To our surprise, the driver stopped and, when we told him where we were heading, he said he was going near Stafford. He said that two of us could get in the cab and the other two would have to go in the back of the van. There was a shutter door on the side. He opened it, muttered something, we climbed in and he closed the shutter door. The back of the van was loaded with fresh bread and it smelt delicious.

I stood up in the space behind the door and Scouse sat on the bread baskets. Bad mistake! Not only that, he opened one of the loaves and started to eat it. Sometime later the van stopped. The driver went mental when he opened the shutter door.

"I told you two to stand up in the van!" he yelled. So that's what he'd been muttering! The bread Scouse had been sitting on was as flat as a pancake. Like cowards we all ran off, giving no thought as to how the driver would explain his 'pancake bread.'

CHAPTER FORTY-FIVE

THE RIDES FROM HELL

My mate Bobby and I decided to go further afield one day. We had 72-hour passes and decided to hitch to Glasgow.

We got a couple of lifts in cars, including an elderly couple driving an old Austin Seven. The old guy drove like a bat out of hell with his wife saying, "Now John, be careful. You are going too fast!" Bobby and I were terrified in the back. They stopped at a transport café on the A6.

Again we were lucky. There was a lorry loaded with fruit and the driver was going to Glasgow fruit market, just a few miles from where we lived. It was a ten-tonne lorry and it seemed massive to us. I sat beside the driver and Bobby sat beside the door. It was a tight squeeze but it was lovely and warm. It did stink of diesel though. The guy was very chatty and told us all about the transport cafés where you could get bed and breakfast and just about anything else, including sex! Very enlightening. We reached the top of the Shap summit, which was 1,250 feet up. The driver then kicked the lorry out of gear and we went hurtling down the other side. Again, we were terrified. Bobby's knuckles were white from clenching the door handle whilst the driver cheerfully pointed out the gaps in the roadside barriers and told us, "That's where so and so went over last week." If he was trying to scare us he was doing a damn good job. He put the lorry back in gear and we settled down again. This was turning out to be the journey from hell. What with old John the OAP and now the truck driver trying to kill us off, it was enough to put you off hitch hiking for life. We finished off with something to eat at a transport café in Moffat (no longer there, but what great sausage, bacon and egg on Scotch rolls, along with the lovely smell).

CHAPTER FORTY-SIX

TV COMES TO 16 MU

We had a technician called Lofty (for obvious reasons). He told us one day that he was going to build a television, which we all took with a pinch of salt. We certainly had all the bits needed on site. What we couldn't figure out was how he was going to get them off site. Now and again the Special Police would check you out before you got on the lorry to go back to the main camp.

However, we soon found out how Lofty got the bits off site! I was about to get on the wagon one night when I heard a rattling in my great-coat pockets. On investigation, I discovered that they were full of resistors and compactors, together with some valves. I said nothing. Then I found out that the rest of our crew had more of the same in their pockets! Just as well we weren't searched or we would all have been in the dock.

How Lofty ever managed to get a cathode ray tube off the site is beyond me, but he did. He then built a fully working nine-inch television, much to our amazement. He admitted that he had filled our pockets with various bits and pieces and was quite sure we wouldn't get caught. I didn't share his belief and checked my pockets from then on, but I must admit he was a very clever chap!

CHAPTER FORTY-SEVEN

AN EXTRA DAY'S LEAVE

As you ex-servicemen will know, people were always on the lookout for thinking up little scams. A Scottish lad told us that if you lived in a remote part of Scotland you were entitled to two days extra travelling time. As Bobby and I lived in Glasgow we were not due any extra time. However the lad told us that if we came up with some name that was not on the map it wouldn't be challenged. We applied for leave and the Duty Sergeant asked us where we were going to.

"Auchenshuggle," we said. (Yes it's a real name, it's a district in Glasgow.) He said he had never heard of it, not surprisingly, and we got our extra two days!

CHAPTER FORTY-EIGHT

FOOTBALL GETS ME INTO TROUBLE AGAIN!

I always enjoyed my leave, during which I visited the youth club. I found out that the football team were playing in a cup final the day after my leave expired. I said I wouldn't have minded playing in that. Ian Drummonds said, "Well now's your chance. Our right back is injured and you would make a ready replacement." Like an idiot I said I would play. Little did I realise what I had let myself in for, especially as we lost the match.

I travelled back to camp and went straight to the sick bay where I had a friend who said he would register me as reporting sick the day before and I would be okay. A couple of weeks went by and then Mr Appleton said that my presence was required at the Orderly Room. I reported to the Duty Sergeant and he said, "It's about your leave, lad."

Oh no, I thought, I've been rumbled.

The Duty Sergeant told me that I had been a day late reporting back. I said I wasn't and had reported sick the day I was due back. "No problem, I will just phone and check," he said. He came off the phone with a big grin on his face. "You're in trouble, lad. There's no record of you going sick on that date." My idiot friend! He had forgotten to book me in. I was formally charged with being AWOL (absent without leave). I had to appear before a Squadron Leader, who read out a list of charges. They were as follows:-

- Absent without leave for one week (one day surely?)
- Breaking into and out of camp for one week.
- Depriving another airman of his rations for one week.
- Conduct prejudice to the good order of His Majesty the King.

I was gobsmacked! How could one day turn into a week? The Squadron Leader told me I had only been found out after two weeks and as Mr Appleton had confirmed that I had actually been on 3 Site for those two weeks and was of good character, they would overlook the second week! I protested and said I would admit to one day AWOL, but not two weeks.

He said, "Very well. You are sentenced to seven days confinement to barracks." (What would I have got for two weeks?) "Do you accept my punishment? If not, I will refer you to the CO." I said I would accept, after all, what hardship would there be in staying in camp for a week. How little did I know?

CHAPTER FORTY-NINE

'JANKERS'

Jankers was a term used to describe punishment for disobeying rules and regulations, as prescribed in Standing Orders. I was told to report to the main Guards Room after work at 18:00 hours. It was then explained what CB (confinement to barracks) meant – no privileges, i.e. sport, cinema, NAAFI, and you had to report every night at 18:00 hours in full kit, suitably blancoed, and buttons, boots and cap badge gleaming, or else! Any infringement of these rules and you would receive further punishment. On top of this bull-shit (which I thought I had left behind in Hereford) you had to carry out certain duties.

The first night after inspection, myself and another Scotsman were told to report to the Guards Room at the other end of camp. We were told we would be sleeping there, and every morning we would have to give an early call to the cooks and catering staff as well as any Duty Officers who were on call. The other Scotsman (known as Jock) told me he was trying to work his ticket. In other words, he was doing his best to try and get booked out of the RAF. He was a regular and still had another five years to do. He would appear on parade with items of kit missing, no laces in his boots, silly things like wearing his beret back to front and, of course, he would be charged over and over again, thus extending the period of Jankers. He thought it was a great laugh and would pay off eventually. I thought he was mad and this turned out to be true!

The two corporals in the Guards Room were quite decent for Special Police. On about the third night, Jock asked if we could go to the NAAFI for a short break. The corporal said it wasn't allowed. Jock begged and pleaded, saying we were bored and it would only be for a cup of tea and a cake and that we would be straight back. We were told to tidy up the Guard Room and then we could go for no more than half an hour.

Duties completed, we went to the NAAFI. As soon as we got there, Jock booked us on to the snooker table.

"Are you mad?" I asked him (of course he was). "We were told half an hour."

"Oh, don't worry about it. He won't do anything about it. He's scared of me, they all are," he said.

Like an idiot I stayed with him. Truth be told I was a bit wary of him myself. We got back to the Guard Room about two hours later. The corporal was furious. "Where were you?" he demanded.

"Playing snooker, what's it to you?" said Jock.

The Special Police officer said, "You're in serious trouble now," which was what Jock wanted.

"Oh well," he said. "In for a penny in for a pound," and promptly landed a punch on the Special Police officer which sent him flying backwards into the stove, as a result of which the chimney came down. The scene was like something out of a wild west film or Laurel and Hardy. The other corporal came in and, between them, they managed to restrain him, put him in a cell and later he was picked up by the Special Police from the main Guards Room. I never saw or heard about him again so I don't know if he did manage to work his ticket.

After he had been taken away I thought, "I'm in for it now." I thought I would probably be charged as well, but I was told that I wouldn't be as it was all Jock's fault. I served the rest of my time without any trouble and was never in trouble after that.

CHAPTER FIFTY

MOTHER STRIKES AGAIN

As I told you at the beginning of my story, my mother had tried to stop me being called up, which was bad enough. The next trick she pulled was really evil. Before she pulled this one I had been called to the CO's office (I was getting to know him well!).

"Can you read and write, lad?" he said.

"Of course I can," I said.

"Very well," he said, and gave me a notepad and pen, saying, "Now you can write to your mother and tell her you are alive and well. She has written to me and said she hasn't heard from you for six months!" True, I never was and still am not a good letter writer. I was really embarrassed. I finished the letter and the CO told me to leave it and he would see that it got posted. I wouldn't have minded, but I had been on leave at least twice and she knew I was okay!

However, what she did next was really appalling. A telegram was sent to the CO saying: "Your mother is dying. Come home at once." Once again I stood in front of the CO. He arranged leave, ration money and a car to take me to the station for the 12.15 train to Glasgow, all within half an hour. All the way home I was worried sick. Lo and behold, when I got home, there was no sign in the dining room of either my mother or father. I thought she had been taken to hospital, but I should have known better. A short time later they both appeared, quite surprised to see me. They had been out shopping.

I was really angry and demanded to know what the hell my mother was thinking about. To be fair, she had suffered on and off with depression and I think she had been in a depressed mood when she had done this. I was surprised at my dad for letting this happen though, but then again he was a very much an 'anything for a quiet life' sort of man.

I stayed for a couple of days and had to go back and lie to the CO saying that my mother was on the mend, thanked him for his concern and crossed my fingers that she wouldn't try anything silly again. I only had ten months left to do. Those ten months however turned out to be quite eventful.

CHAPTER FIFTY-ONE

SCARLET FEVER

I came home on leave at Christmas and was not due back until after New Year. We were at a mate's house on New Year's Eve (Hogmanay). It was a bitter cold night. There was a coal fire burning and the room was lovely and warm. We were playing cards and having a laugh and had arranged to go to a party after the bells at midnight.

I got warmer and warmer as the night wore on and one of my mates said, "You look like a red Indian."

I laughed and said that I felt really warm - by this time I was boiling.

"It's not that warm," they said. I went home at 10.00 pm and told my parents that I was going to lie down for a bit and asked them to wake me before midnight so that I could see the New Year in with them and then go back out. Go out I did, in a big way!

The next thing I remember is lying down and looking up at a white ceiling with bright lights on it and a voice saying, "Can you touch the roof with your foot? Good, now the other one." If this was a dream it was a cracker. I came round a bit and was told I was on my way to the Fever Hospital (they thought I might have Rheumatic Fever), which was quite serious (was my mother's plan working at last?). Apparently my parents had tried to waken me at home, but couldn't. When they realised I was burning up, the doctor was called and, when he saw me, rang for an ambulance (the white roof and bright lights). There would be another ambulance later, a military one, but more of that later.

I was admitted to the fever ward in isolation in Belvidere Hospital (in 1963 our first born was delivered there). I was diagnosed with scarlet fever and injected with penicillin every four hours for the next few days. The incubation period was about fourteen to twenty-one days so I must have had it prior to going on leave.

I was told that I would be in isolation for at least ten days or more and another week in the convalescence ward before I would be allowed out. It was not all unpleasant. After all, anything was better than the boredom of Stafford!

After ten days I was allowed into the other ward and told to keep away from the fever ward otherwise I could get infected again. The nurses in both wards were great. One day I was asked to go into the fever ward for some dinner plates (well, not asked, I volunteered). A couple of days later the doctor came round and examined me.

"What's this rash on his stomach and his scalp? Has he been in contact with the fever ward?" he asked. He was assured no. "Well, he has been re-infected." I had scarletina, a mild form of scarlet fever, and so I was shipped back to the fever ward for another week or so. The doctor was furious, but I couldn't snitch on the nurses and I was adamant that I hadn't been in contact with the fever ward! So what was supposed to be seven days' leave was turning out to be a rather extended stay in hospital.

During my time in Belvidere I was visited by a Warrant Officer from Cowglen Military Hospital. He was there to check on my progress and also to give me my pay and ration money, which apparently I was entitled to during my stay. We had a German matron on our ward and she stood no nonsense from anyone. The Warrant Officer came back after I had been put back in the other ward having recovered and been given the all clear. In his opinion the Warrant Officer believed that I was fit to travel and I would have to report back to my unit the next day.

"How dare you come into my ward and tell this young man he is fit to travel," the matron said. "Get out of here and don't come back. We will let you know when he is fit and well."

The Warrant Officer left with his tail between his legs!

CHAPTER FIFTY-TWO

WE COULDN'T FIND HIM SIR!

My time was running down and I had about four months left to do. In the main I enjoyed my time, but it was only the fact that I had made some good friends and the people I worked with were good company too. Nevertheless, the sheer boredom was hard to take and I would much rather have been at home. I had very little leave left, but I took three days and went home. I did not try the 'Auchenshuggle' trick again though!

Whilst on leave I went into the café where we all used to meet up before we went dancing or to the pictures or football. I was the only one of us away on National Service. One of my friends worked in the shipyards and was exempt. The other two were Grade Four! I went into the café one night and there was a lad there in the army, who hated it. He said he had a cunning plan to get more leave. Someone told him if you went to your doctor and told him you were too ill to travel he would give you a sick note to extend your leave. This idea appealed to me. Little did I know that he had tried this trick, said he had pains in his stomach and the doctor sent him straight to hospital where they whisked out his appendix! He got his extra leave all right, but at a price.

Not knowing all of this until much later, I presented myself at the doctor's and told him I was unwell and had pains in my side. I had suffered from kidney trouble and pleurisy when I was five years old and didn't go to school until I was six (hence the reason my mother insisted that I was delicate and was over protective when I was growing up and in much later life, as you have seen). The doctor examined me and said in his opinion I was okay to travel and so I prepared to travel back the next day. Unbeknown to me he had phoned the RAF base at Bishopbriggs and arranged for me to go there and be checked over just in case!

I went to the pictures with my mate, Morry. When I got home at about 10.30 pm my dad was jumping about - not his usual demeanour at all!

"Where have you been?" he demanded.

"At the pictures," I said.

"There was an RAF ambulance here to pick you up about 8.00 pm and I didn't know where you were." I knew he wasn't kidding. Well you don't about something like that do you? "You do realise the MPs will come and arrest you?" said my dad. "What were you thinking?" I told him that I was just trying to get a few more days' leave. "You'll be lucky if they don't lock you up for months!" he replied.

I spent the night waiting for the knock. It came at around 08.30, not from MPs, but in the form of an ambulance with a big red cross on the roof, which I could see from my bedroom window. I saw two lads get out carrying a stretcher. My dad let them in and I recognised one of them. He was in the Youth Club with us.

"I suppose I'm in trouble now," I said to him.

"No," he said. "We told the Medical Officer we couldn't find your house in the fog." It was true about the fog. It was quite bad the night before! "He told us to come back this morning." I was told to hop on to the stretcher so we could get going.

I laughed and said, "You're joking, I'm fine."

"We know, but it will look good for the neighbours!" he said.

So I hopped on to the stretcher for a second time and I was carried out of the house and into the ambulance. We went off to RAF Bishopbriggs, the place the kindly old officer at Hereford had told me I would be going to!

On arrival I was taken into a sickbay and examined by a Medical Officer, a young man who was very sympathetic to National Servicemen (just as well for me). He referred me to Cowglen Military Hospital, where I was given an injection by the biggest needle I have ever seen!

I was then x-rayed and taken back to Bishopbriggs to await the results, which came back negative and I thought that would be that.

I was wrong! The officer had a chat with me and I told him about Stafford and my dislike of the place. He told me to get back into bed and he would see what he could do about keeping me for a bit. There were about five other bods in the ward and it was obvious that none of us were very ill. The MO came round in the morning and announced that we were all fit to travel. We had our breakfast and then the orderly said that those of us who lived locally could go home, but to be back in the morning before 07:00 hours for the MO's inspection. So I did this for about a week, but then he told us he couldn't cover for us anymore. Never mind, he had done me a favour by ringing the camp. My dad couldn't believe what was going on and said I would probably have been shot in the First World War for malingering (as if). I returned to Stafford where I now only had three months to go and I was getting 'demob happy.'

CHAPTER FIFTY-THREE

FIRE PICKET

Because we worked in AIS we were excused duties such as Fire Picket where you patrolled the site at night as security and had to spot any likely fires. The sergeant at the Orderly Office had tried his best to get us doing Fire Picket, but was always told by Mr Appleton that his boys could be posted overseas at any moment, much to the sergeant's annoyance.

Taylor and I were in the stores one day collecting our laundry, which was done by a Chinese laundry and a great job they did of it too (especially the shirt collars). Anyway, the Sergeant said, "What are your two's service numbers?" We told him and his face lit up. "So you have less than three months to do then and can't be posted anywhere," he said. Thus we found ourselves on Fire Picket duty for a week solid.

We had a quiet four nights and saw no-one and nothing untoward. On the last night Taylor and I saw this staff car come through the gates at about midnight and an officer got out and looked around. I said to Taylor to go to the back of the hanger and, if the officer came over to me, to come up behind him quietly. The officer saw me standing alone and came running over, shouting, "I could overpower you. You shouldn't be on your own. I could have a bomb here and blow the whole hanger up."

I saw Taylor behind him and said, "Look behind you, Sir." He turned round and saw Taylor with hands like shovels and his night stick poised ready to strike (a night stick was all we had to protect us).

"Well done chaps. I was just testing you!" he said.

CHAPTER FIFTY-FOUR

AND SO THE END IS NEAR

I still had a fair few experiences to come, like going to the Band in the Wall dance hall with Ginger on his motorbike. On the return journey he hit something in the road and we were both thrown off the bike. I was wearing a heavy duty leather body warmer that my dad used to wear on the trams when it was cold. I also had a pair of sheepskin gauntlets on. I slid along the road on my front and all the buttons on my coat were ripped off and the palms of the gauntlets were torn out. Apart from a few grazes though, I was okay. Ginger wasn't so lucky. He had a broken leg and was in dock for a few weeks. They say the pillion passenger gets the worst of it, so I must have been very lucky!

The other experience was a sad one. A Jewish lad we knew was thrown from the back of a lorry and died from his injuries. I only mention this because I learned something from it. We went to the funeral and took a wreath with us. We found out to our horror that you take fruit to a Jewish funeral and not flowers.

I was invited to spend Christmas with another lad and had a very nice time. I was very touched when his little sister gave me a small present wrapped in Christmas paper. It was a packet of razor blades. I wanted to return the hospitality and invited the lad to spend the New Year with me.

"Do you live near the Gorbals?" he asked.

"Not too far away," I said.

"I'm sorry," he said, "I don't want to come and get beaten up or slashed with a razor!"

I tried to tell him that this wouldn't happen, but somebody must have filled his head with nonsense and he wouldn't come.

The other pleasant experience I had was when Mr Appleton asked me to babysit for him and his wife during the last couple of months.

He picked me up in his car, laid on a drink and sandwiches and cakes and gave me a few bob on top. His son was no trouble at all and I quite enjoyed it.

It was the custom when a lad got demobbed they had a party in a pub (I didn't drink so I just went quietly). I attended one such party in the Grapes in Stafford. I had what I thought were a couple of shandies and left the pub to catch the last bus, which I missed. By this time I felt quite drunk. Somebody, no doubt thinking it was funny, had spiked my drinks. Stafford Prison has a huge wall that runs for about two or three miles on the road to the camp. In my drunken state I had a flash of inspiration. I would lean on the wall and follow it all the way back to camp. It must have worked because I woke up the next morning feeling very rough and my shoes and the bottom of my trousers were covered in mud. Here ended lesson one – don't get drunk and not know what you are doing!

It was also a custom when a lad got demobbed to put things he didn't want on the table in the hope of selling them. Scouse was getting out and among the things he was getting rid of was a mouth-organ. I asked him what he wanted for it and he said 2/6 (12 ½ pence).

"No, I'll give you one shilling for it," I offered him. It lay there all day and he kept asking me for 2/6, dropping to 2/ and eventually to 1/6 and I just replied, "No, one shilling."

It was still there at the end of the day and I got it for a shilling! I couldn't play the thing and every time I tried to play it I had boots and shoes thrown at me along with verbal abuse! I stuck at it, abuse and all, and finally I could play 'God save the King' (yes the King was still alive. He died before I was demobbed and the Queen took over, so I can say I served King and Queen). I still play the chromatic harmonica to this day, but I don't get as much abuse as I used to!

I had one week to go and I was minding my own business when I passed a young Pilot Officer. He called me over and said, "That forage cap is disgusting and your collar is badly frayed," (which was true).

I told him I was getting demobbed the following week, but he said, "I don't care, get them replaced and report to me when you have done so." I had to go to the stores and get a new collar and a beret, for forage caps were now obsolete. I also had to pay for them - all for a week's service. I reported back to the officer and he was satisfied that I had replaced them.

I was tempted to say, "Get some in," to him, but I didn't. The beret was awful and despite trying to shrink it in cold water it still looked like a 'pea on a drum' when I wore it. It suffered the same fate as my two uniforms, which were put in a cupboard and forgotten about when I got home. It's a good job I wasn't called up from the reserve list (the Z men) which you were on for eight years after being demobbed. When I finally checked them after two years they were totally moth eaten, including the beret!

CHAPTER FIFTY-FIVE

FINALLY, DEMOB TIME

The day arrived when I was finally demobbed. I had my kit bag packed and my final leave pass and pay, together with my ration money and discharge papers in my pocket. After all the trials and tribulations, the discharge papers read:-

Samuel Reilly Official Number 3130146 A.C.I.

- Christian Names: Samuel
- Period of Service from: 31.10.50 – 24.11.52
- RAF Trade: Admin Orderly
- Trade Training: None
- Description of Duties: grading of radio equipment by visual inspection under supervision

Assessment of Conduct, Proficiency and Personal Qualities:-

- Conduct: Exemplary
- Ability as Tradesman: Good
- Leadership: Fairly Good
- Co-operation: Good
- Bearing: Smart
- Remarks: a good tradesman who, although possessing no special qualifications, has shown interest in his duties

Signed: A. O. Budd, Wing Commander

And so at last I could walk out the main gate a free man (almost). Another lad and I walked out together and when we got clear of the gates we turned round and gave the 'V' sign to the camp! We were spotted by a Special Policeman and told to come back. He reminded us that we were not officially demobbed until our leave ended on 25 November 1952!

It just shows it pays to check your documents, especially your discharge papers. He said we could still be charged with making obscene gestures. He let us off and we piled on to a waiting Midland Red bus and then on to the train home.

After all these years I still have mixed feelings about National Service. Yes it taught me to stand on my own two feet, but it had an unsettling effect for quite a while trying to adapt to civvy street and my old job in a warehouse.

I did object and still do at being called up at the age of eighteen with no right to vote or have a drink until I was twenty-one. Yet I was trained to kill or be killed. That didn't make sense to me! I know that the law has changed now and you can vote and drink officially at the age of eighteen. The sorrow is that young men are still being killed in their hundreds - for what? Wars that no-one wants. I don't suppose things will change anytime soon.

I did feel a bit of a cheat some years later when I was presented with my Veterans badge by Tom Watson, M.P. I felt that I hadn't really earned it, but on the other hand I did serve my country for two years. I felt that the present-day young men who are being killed or wounded are more deserving of recognition than we were (my opinion). What the badge did prove was that I had "got some in" and no one can take that away from me.

I have been demobbed for almost fifty nine years now and married for fifty three with a supportive wife and family and grandchildren. I would support the return of National Service, but only to replace prison sentences (or lack of them) for the young thugs who terrorise our society today – a real "Bad Lad's Army" if you like – and teach them some discipline and respect for other people, which is sadly missing today. That's me off my soap box now!

I hope those of you who "got some in" and have read my account of my own service and even those who only stand and watch have enjoyed my journey through National Service and it will re-kindle (pun intended) some memories of your own.

--- *3130146 Aircraftsman First Class Reilly. S* (or 'Eventually' as Warrant Officer Appleton told me he called me on the day I left the section because, as he said, "We would ask you to do something and you did 'eventually'."). All that time and I never knew I had a nickname!

Also by Samuel Reilly

"Can You Come Back Next Week?"

Often amusing, laugh out loud funny in parts, sometimes thought-provoking, and occasionally tear jerking, "Can You Come Back Next Week?" is an account of one young collector/salesman's exploits and adventures selling goods on credit door to door in the poorer areas of Glasgow in the 50s and 60s. If you lived through those times, you will find memories galore in these words, and for those who did not, it proves an evocative glimpse into a time past, where a radiogram which loaded ten records at once was the height of luxury, to be paid for scrupulously week on week, even though your kids ran around in vests and bare bums. Set upon by a sword-wielding maniac, dangled from a twenty-first storey balcony, and being offered it "on a plate" in lieu of payment – life in the Credit Trade was certainly never dull!

"Play Days, Childhood and Other Things"

I wonder how many people remember their childhood. I mean, really remember. I suppose it depends on whether it was a happy or miserable time! We all like to think we do.

In writing about these memories which took place over fifty years ago I've had to delve deep into the recesses of my mind to conjure up what, to me, were happy childhood days (the mind has its own way of closing off the bad times) despite the fact that six years of them were tainted by the Second Great War that was never supposed to happen again.

In recalling these memories I hope to take you through many happy and, sometimes, sad times and perhaps stir some thoughts which will recapture some of your own childhood days!

Printed in Great Britain
by Amazon